WHAT PEOPLE ARE SAYING ABOUT
FATHERHOOD FACEPLANTS

"It's time to stop faking our way through fatherhood. Being a better dad begins by letting God father us first. Through personal stories of humor, regret, and hope, Troy reveals how he went from a wreck of a man to a healthy dad—and how we can do the same."

Allen Arnold, Executive Producer of Content, Wild at Heart,
Author of *Chaos Can't* and *The Story of With*

"*Fatherhood Faceplants* is both a story of one man's life and a practical guidebook for the rest of us men. Troy Mangum is a storyteller with a giant heart. His writing is a rare and powerful combination of vulnerability and optimism. He knows firsthand the depth and width of God's goodness and love because he's experienced them in dark moments of heartbreak and regret and in soaring moments of wonder and glory. Don't miss this opportunity to benefit from Troy's hard-fought wisdom."

Justin Camp, Founder of Wire for Men, Author of *Invention* and *Odyssey*,
and Co-founder Gather Ministries

"Don't let the title mislead you. This book is an invitation to ALL men, not just fathers. In these pages lies an invitation for every man, husband, son, father, brother, and grandfather. An invitation to become fully alive by becoming fully known. An invitation to find strength by embracing weakness.

I warn you. This book is fiercely vulnerable and bold. I don't know any other way to say it than this, this book gives you permission to embrace uncertainty, weakness, and the unknown. Why? Because you were never called to be the hero. God is the hero. And when we live from that truth... we become men of valor and strength. We become the men that our families, our spouses, our children, our grandchildren, our friends, and the world are waiting for."

Jeremy Robertson, Lead Pastor, Vertical Life Church

"What a journey full of treasures! As a not-yet father, this book has reminded me to slow down and pay attention to my own faceplants and victories as God gradually uncovers who He has made me to be. The treasures in these pages helped me focus on living as a son, a husband, and one-day father. Troy reminds us that God tends to invite us into the arena- to ask, rather than tell, offer rather than command, as we walk through this road of life . . . that way, through the faceplants, we join WITH our Heavenly Father, in taking and owning ground together. This is a brutally candid and beautifully courageous invitation to journey with God as a Father. I appreciate this rare glimpse into the guts and the glory of the adventure called life in the Father's Kingdom. This book is a call to us all to go further in and farther up!"

J. David Weiss, Super Yacht Designer, Entrepreneur,
Alchemist/Arsonist of Creativity

"Troy Mangum has written a beautifully vulnerable book about the journey of rejection and failure that most men know well, but few can share. Many of us hide it well enough until we have kids. But at that point, the charade is over, and most fathers need help. Mangum shows us how to face our failures and shame with courage. He shows us how to begin to walk in freedom. If you want to give your kids the greatest gift they'll ever receive, read *Fatherhood Faceplants*, take notes, and do what it says."

Seth Barnes, Founder of Adventures in Missions and the World Race,
Author of *Kingdom Journeys* and *The Art of Listening Prayer*

"Vulnerable and strong, authentic and powerful. In Troy Mangum's new book *Fatherhood Faceplants*, he explores the depths of pain many fathers face and the redemptive purposes of our loving Father God who works all things together for our good. Thanks for sharing your journey with us, Troy, and for inspiring every dad to be the man God created them to be."

Matt Tommey, Artist, Mentor, Speaker,
and Author of *The Thriving Christian Artist*,
Voted "Best Art Mentors" by *Professional Artist Magazine* in 2018

"The young addict sat, head down wringing his hands. I drove him to the recovery ministry. The man who interviewed the lost boy asked the most penetrating question: 'Do you want to grow up and be a man?' Without looking up, in shame, the addicted boy motioned a feeble yes. Then the man asked the boy, 'Do you even know what a man is? A man does what needs to be done regardless of the cost, while a boy does what he wants to do regardless of the need.

Troy Mangum wrote *Fatherhood Faceplants* to help boys become men—fathers! He shares stories from his own journey, which led him, a boy, to become a man—a MAN OF GOD—which is what a true father is."

Ken Helser, Musician, Artist, Storyteller,
Founder of "A Place for the Heart"

"*Fatherhood Faceplants* is not a book containing all the ways that Troy Mangum (and every other dad who has ever lived) had failed in his role as a dad. And whilst it does offer the essential understanding of why we dads did or do fail our children at times . . . specifically because we were first wounded ourselves as sons . . . it offers the reader so much more. *Fatherhood Faceplants* is a book that outlines the path and the process of restoration and transformation of entire family units."

Darren Lewis, Founder, Facilitator,
and Fatherhood Coach of "Fathering Adventures"–Australia

FATHERHOOD FACEPLANTS

HOW TO GET BACK UP AND BE THE DAD YOUR KIDS NEED

CREATOR OF THE KINDLING FIRE PODCAST

TROY MANGUM

DEDICATION

To my beautiful wife, Kathy. I love you with all my heart.
I would not be the man I am today without your love,
wisdom, straight talk, and laughter.

To my four children: Rayn, Avi, Olin, and Abrie.
I love you so much.
You are Mighty! Ps. 112:2
The best is yet to come!

To my dad, for showing me how to never quit!

CONTENTS

Foreword 1

Introduction 3

ALL DADS FACEPLANT

Chapter 1: Boyhood, Not All It's Cracked Up to Be. 11

Chapter 2: Meeting God on Acid. 17

Chapter 3: Wait, I'm Not Ready to Be a Dad 27

Chapter 4: On the Brink of Death 39

Chapter 5: The Beginning of the End 53

GETTING BACK UP

Chapter 6: Stop Hitting Yourself 63

Chapter 7: A Literal Sign from God. 69

Chapter 8: Trust Big, Go Low 73

Chapter 9: Home Again 79

TRAINING FOR WAR

Chapter 10: Leave the American Dream 87

Chapter 11: Play the Long Game. 105

Chapter 12: Be a Lover and a Fighter 111

Chapter 13: Face Your Battles 121

A VICTORIOUS LEGACY

Chapter 14: Repair the Breach 137

Chapter 15: Live Uncovered. 145

Chapter 16: Run Free 151

Chapter 17: Be Awesome 159

Acknowledgments 167

About the Author. 169

FOREWORD

IT WAS A FALL DAY, THE KIND THAT TELLS YOU WINTER IS COMING. THE weatherman says it'll be "cloudy and cold." At one time, you might've described Troy Mangum's heart the same way: cloudy and cold.

I met Troy in a parking lot several minutes before a seven a.m. weekly men's group. I was early so I could get things set up and the all-important coffee on. Troy rolled down his window and asked, "Is this where the Wednesday Morning Group meets?" He looked like a guy who had spent the night in his car. I let him know he was in the right place. He got out of his car and, like a stray, followed me inside for warmth and maybe a meal. So began my eleven-year friendship with Troy.

After that first meeting, Troy came up and asked, "Would you have some time to grab coffee? I'd really like to talk." He asked one of my favorite questions. Over the next several months, I heard his story. Separated from his wife and kids because of the pain he was causing. Starting to see how events from boyhood were affecting him and his family today.

He did not realize it at the time, but he was at the beginning of an incredible comeback story!

Fatherhood is a tough road. For most of us, it is an unmarked and uncharted frontier. Like marriage, it is one of those major life shift moments when you enter the door one thing and exit it another. With marriage, you walk away a husband with a wife. With fatherhood, you walk away a dad and your world has changed drastically, again. Both roles: husband and father, will eventually shake a man down to his core.

In his book, *Fatherhood Faceplants*, my friend Troy Mangum offers his story and the lessons learned along the way for other dads to discover. He details how God fathered him to become a man his wife and children could count on to love them.

And there's the trick . . . Fatherhood is an on-the-job training program. A circus of trials and errors, some more painful and expensive than others.

In a day and time where there are lots of voices: instructors and teachers . . . experts telling us "how-to," Troy actually tells stories from his life of how *not* to and why.

There is a reason many roads have warning signs posted by dangerous spots—because someone got hurt there and was kind enough to leave behind some guidance. Troy has paid the price for his words and stories in *Fatherhood Faceplants*. They were expensive and, therefore, he believes he might be able to encourage a few of us along our own road of fatherhood.

Thank you, Troy, for sharing your story and the invitation for a few more of us strays to find some warmth and maybe a meal in the circle of fatherhood—where we are learning how to have our own comeback story.

Michael Thompson
Founder of Zoweh Ministries,
author of *Heart of a Warrior*

INTRODUCTION

"DO ALL DADDIES HAVE TO LEAVE?"

OUR MARRIAGE COUNSELOR GAVE UP ON US. HE TOLD US HE WAS DONE. When the person who is trying to help you says it is hopeless, that is not good. After eight months of separation, the future of the family Kathy and I had made did not look bright.

I saw my kids every other weekend. I lived in a sparsely furnished apartment two miles from my house. It felt like a million.

As a Christian dad, I tried to keep us all together, but it fell apart. After fourteen years of wreaking havoc on my home, it finally caught up to me.

On the same day that our marriage counselor gave up on us, Kathy called to tell me our youngest daughter Abrie had lice, and she thought she may have it too. Would I come over, check her, and bring them dinner?

Like a stranger, I walked up to my house and rang the doorbell. The last time I was home had been four months earlier, on Christmas day. After checking Kathy for lice and eating dinner as a family, I got to put my youngest children, Olin and Abrie, to bed.

I went upstairs for the first time in four months. Going up the steps with the paint and stain I'd applied years ago, hearing the same old creaks from happier times, walking down the hall, past the broken folding door that kept our washer and dryer hidden, I thought, *I never did get a chance to fix that door.*

I walked into Abrie's bedroom, spying her bob haircut and sparkling eyes peeking out from the top of the covers. "I came up to say good-night and pray with you like we used to." Words came out in prayers that slipped from my memory. My heart was heavy. Then Abrie prayed to God that "Daddy would come home." Tears welled up in my eyes. Not knowing what to say, I managed to get out an "amen." I awkwardly told her good-night, hugged her, then headed to Olin's room, wiping tears from my eyes.

I sat on his bed, running my hand over his hair, looking into his innocent face. I moved my hand to his shoulder and began to pray. When it was Olin's time to add his prayers, he stopped and looked up at me. "Daddy, why did you leave us?" My tears began to fall freely. My memory is blank on how I responded. Continuing to look at me with the saddest eyes, he asked, "Do all daddies have to leave?"

At six and four, Olin and Abrie did not understand the complexities that led to their parents splitting up. I could not rewind the time and take back fourteen years of failure. The damage had been done.

I could have really used a book like this when I was a young married man trying to figure out family life. I'd figured out most of my life on my own but was weary and failing. I desperately needed a male role model who had gone before and could help me navigate the pitfalls of being a dad. Someone to guide me on overcoming the demons that haunted me.

All I wanted was a dad.

Wherever I turned, it seemed other couples knew how to have a happy marriage and kids. What was wrong with me? How was I supposed to know how to be something I was never taught or modeled?

Do dads need a dad? Yes, we do.

When we faceplant, we need someone there to pick us up. A simple definition of a faceplant is an epic failure that occurs while attempting a daring feat, such as raising children.

I wanted to do better. I wanted to be better. Yet, destructive patterns kept recurring in my marriage and parenting. It was time for me to figure this out.

To all you men out there who were like me, trying to figure this out on your own, you don't have to. This book is for you. Maybe you are a dad in your twenties who is worried about having kids. Or a dad in your thirties or forties in the middle of raising kids but feels you could be better.

Know this, you are not alone.

You may feel the pain of regret and failure of "screwing up your kids." The message I hope you find in my story is that you can become the dad your kids need. You can rise above failures, shortcomings, and sin.

In God's family, fathers still have a dad to go to. We are not left to figure everything out on our own. As grown men, it is hard to recognize how God is fathering us. Yet seeing His work in our lives is the key to turning our family around for the better.

What does it look like to have God fathering us?

This book is my journey of God being a dad to me. As you read, I hope you will start to recognize God in your own life, fathering you.

The weekend before our counselor gave up on us, I was at a men's retreat in the Virginia mountains. The retreat was called "Heart of a Warrior" and was put on by Zoweh Ministries. During the retreat, we spent time alone with God asking Him questions, listening for His answers. I asked God, "How can You love me when I have been so terrible to my wife and kids?" He told me, "I am a perfect Father whose love never changes based on your behavior."

Then He asked me a question. (You know it's about to go down when God asks you a question.)

"Do you not discipline your children because you love them? When their hearts turn from rebellious to broken and contrite, do they not know you still love them?" Yes, when my kids respond to correction and I embrace them, they know their dad loves them deeply.

Then God said, "You have evidence of My love because I discipline you. You are not an orphan. Your worth is found in belonging to Me, not in what you can or cannot do."

5

This Bible verse came to mind: "The Lord disciplines the one he loves, and he chastens everyone he accepts as his son" (Heb 12:6, NIV).

God had an honest father-son conversation with me on that Virginia mountainside. He held up a mirror for me to see, for the first time, myself as I truly was: a frightened boy, a cruel husband, and an angry father. Yet God never removed His deep love and affection for me. I did not deserve it. The more truth He brought, the more love I felt.

That day, fighting God and my circumstances stopped. I finally yielded to His loving correction. Then something unexpected happened.

My underlying anger stopped. Emotional instability stopped. Aggressive and argumentative interactions with Kathy stopped. My kids did not feel afraid to be around me as I started responding in a consistent, loving way to normal life versus explosive anger with any little infraction. A safe place was created for my wife and kids—emotionally, physically, mentally, and spiritually—because I became a safe person. We started to enjoy each other's company again.

Regret gave way to peace. Tears gave way to laughter.

The circumstances did not change; I did.

It did not happen overnight. Facing the truth as God revealed it was the first step in Him fathering me. What you hold in your hands are the lessons He taught me along my fatherhood journey.

We all fail as dads. Not one is immune to faceplants. The difference between the dad who becomes who our kids need and the dad filled with regret is how we get back up.

I plan to show you how God helped me get back up, taking me from a wreck of a man to a whole, healthy, and healed dad.

On this journey we will explore how our personal victories become our children's inheritance. How humility comes before honor. How to fight for our family. How to train our children in spiritual warfare. How to stop the tide of generational sin and start a new legacy. How to overcome dad guilt. How to make good decisions that positively affect generations to come. How to create an environment of freedom and peace within our home. How bold dads raise bold kids. How family achievement is more fulfilling than personal achievement.

I cannot wait to see you take back the ground you have lost because of fatherhood faceplants and become the dad your kids need. Let's get rollin'.

ALL DADS FACEPLANT

CHAPTER 1

BOYHOOD, NOT ALL IT'S CRACKED UP TO BE

GOD COMFORTS THE HURTING

THE CRANBERRY SAUCE SPATTERED AGAINST THE DINING-ROOM wall. It was like a murder scene out of a movie. My dad had just picked up the crystal bowl and smashed it against the wall. My mother was screaming and crying next to him.

Welcome to Thanksgiving at the Mangum house.

I come from a long line of fatherhood faceplants. My father had explosive anger issues. His father was neglectful and quiet.

The only story I know of my grandfather was that he spent his time at home, alone on the front porch behind a newspaper, chain-smoking cigarettes. He did not interact much with his five kids as I understand it except for my dad's favored older brother. My father was the proverbial middle child who never gained his father's affection or approval.

With my grandfather's lack of engagement in my dad's life, my grandmother's father stepped in as a positive male role model. They would spend summers together playing checkers and listening to radio dramas like *The Lone Ranger*. He fell in love with the airwaves.

At his grandfather's encouragement, my dad pursued a career in broadcasting and was a radio man until he retired.

My mom is a full-blooded Native American from the Lumbee tribe in North Carolina. My father, a true-blue honky from rural Maryland.

My mom comes from a long line of educators, my grandfather being the first Native American dean of a university in America in the 1930s. She, in turn, pursued a career in education as a school teacher. She retired as an educator and local politician.

My mom and dad met in Pembroke, North Carolina, the home of the Lumbee Indian tribe. My dad's older brother was a Methodist pastor. He moved to the area to do ministry among the Native Americans. My father came to live with his older brother after his broadcast schooling and met my mom there.

At this time in American history, it was considered controversial to have an interracial marriage. They were rebels, apparently. As a young married couple, they moved out to Michigan, Nebraska, Kansas, and Iowa as my dad pursued various radio jobs around the Midwest.

I was born in Lincoln, Nebraska but grew up in Sioux City, Iowa. I'm the youngest in my family. I have one sister, Dawn, who is five years older than me. She was born in Sarnia, Canada, across the border from Port Huron, Michigan. She was my comforter and friend growing up.

I have very few memories of my relationship with my father as I was growing up. I recall two positive memories. One was of me sitting on his lap while he drank Olympia beer watching TV downstairs. I asked him if I could try it, and he let me. The other was watching him build a Sears Roebuck wooden go-kart in the garage for me.

The reality is, I grew up deathly afraid of my father. The incident on Thanksgiving was not just saved for special occasions. Apparently, every day was a holiday in our home.

My father could get violent at any time. I remember his yell would paralyze me in fear. I could not breathe, speak, or run. I was frozen, trapped in my own body with nowhere to hide.

My earliest childhood memory was lying in my bed, terrified. Every night, my dad would start to rage at my mom. I could hear every word from my bedroom. He would punch walls, slam doors, and hit her. His voice sent electric shocks through my little body. I shook in my bed with tears streaming down my face, wondering if at any moment this monster would turn his anger toward me, drag me out of bed, and beat me.

My bedroom door opened, the hallway light shining on my face. I could not see. I could not move. Next thing I knew, my older sister was in bed with me. She was scared too. We held on to each other in love and fear while my father tore apart our home. Night after night. She would stroke my hair and say, "Troy, it's going to be okay." Eventually I would fall asleep with her by my side. But she had no one to comfort her through those long nights.

As I grew, it came time to figure out how to ride a bike. With both Mom and Dad working, I sought to figure it out on my own. My feet barely touched the ground. I tried to find my balance or make forward progress, but the only thing I seemed to know how to do was fall. I wondered how the other boys figured it out so fast. I did not realize, the other boys had help.

Eventually, I caught on, but I was still wobbly. I had a friend in the neighborhood, Toby, who was wild and fun to hang out with. He had a great idea one day. Next to my house was a huge hill that crossed a busy intersection. He said, "Let's ride down the hill on our bikes!" I was in the first grade.

It sounded like a great idea. We walked our bikes up the hill because it was too steep to ride up. Then Toby hopped on his bike and started flying down the hill. I jumped on right behind him.

The wind whipping past me was exhilarating, like nothing I had experienced before. It was pure adrenaline until my friend reached the bottom of the hill. Out of the corner of my eye, I saw it. An army green sedan with a black roof careening right toward my friend. They did not slow down. It all happened so fast.

My friend did not see the car but kept going at full speed. The driver must have seen him at the last second and stomped on the brakes. The screeching sound filled the air, a prelude to the horror that was about to occur. My friend darted in front of the car at full speed, barely avoiding a tragic end.

I could not react fast enough. I slammed on my brakes, sliding on the gravel and dirt that had accumulated at the bottom of the hill. I lost control of my bike. It flew out from underneath me and slid under the front tires of the braking car. A cacophony of crushing metal added to the terror of the moment.

I was flat on my back sliding feetfirst toward the car. My entire body went under the car. My head slamming against the passenger side door is what finally stopped me. I don't remember what happened next.

I was later told the car stopped right before it ran over my chest and killed me. I was rushed to the hospital unconscious. I survived the incident with a concussion and road rash on my back and arms.

A foreshadowing of the many faceplants that would occur throughout my life.

Growing up in Sioux City, Iowa, we were the perfect nuclear family on the outside with two working parents, two children, a yard with a fence, and a cat named Mittens. My mom was an elementary school teacher; my dad a radio station manager for KMNS. From the outside, we were typical.

My mom told me to never speak to my friends about what went on in our house. She tried to keep up appearances, but behind the façade, our home was filled with violence. After years of enduring such pain, thousands of miles away from her family, she decided it was time for all of us to go back to her native North Carolina.

My dad, mom, sister, and I moved near Pembroke, North Carolina, where my grandparents lived, when I was eight and about to start third grade.

My father ended up getting a job in Raleigh, about an hour away. He was the manager at WKIX, a seventies rock radio station. My mom got a job as an elementary school teacher at a local school. We moved into a picture-perfect home in the North Haven subdivision. We were just another white-picket-fence family moving into the neighborhood, but inside our walls, the abuse continued.

TOO WEAK TO RESCUE HER

I had just gotten off the school bus and walked into the kitchen through the garage door. Immediately I sensed something was wrong. I heard screaming and sounds of struggling from the living room. Slowly and quietly, I put my backpack down by the washer and dryer near the door. I crept through the kitchen, around the dinner table, to the doorway of the living room.

In front of the fireplace, next the TV, my mom was laying on the ground. My father, on his knees, towering over her, was hitting her over and over again with his belt. She was screaming, struggling to get free, but he had her pinned. His back was to me, so he did not see me standing in the doorway, but eventually my mom did.

Time stopped as I stood on that threshold. I could not move, look away, or speak. The scene played out in slow motion. The terror and pain on my mother's face was unbearable. We locked eyes. For a moment, she was not alone. We both experienced sadness, compassion, and utter helplessness because we knew an eight-year-old boy could do nothing in this situation but watch.

She pleaded with my dad to stop. She said my name between gasps. She was powerless to make him stop. It must have hurt her even more than my father's blows to watch me take it all in.

My dad turned around and saw me standing there. He looked straight into me with his black eyes and said, "Your mother is very bad." Then he continued beating her with his belt.

He pulled me deep into the tragic scene, crushing me and my heart in one fell swoop.

Too weak to rescue my mother, I stood witnessing the atrocities like a statue. The scene never left me. I have no memory of how it ended. To me, it never really did.

ROBINS

Scenes like these continued in our home until I was ten years old. From my earliest childhood memory back in Iowa through the time I left the house for college, I lived in fear of my father. At any moment, things could spiral out of control. When he came home from work, we never knew what was in store for that evening.

When it got bad, protocol was to exit the house quickly and go out to the front lawn. Meandering around the yard, the sound of muffled yelling came from my house. I occupied the time kicking a soccer ball by myself, working on tricks I had seen Pele, the famous MLS player, do. Bicycle kicks, rainbows, and other moves.

There were always robins in the yard with me, keeping me company. A deep sense of peace would come over me when I saw those birds, as if everything was going to be all right.

CHAPTER 2

MEETING GOD ON ACID

NO ONE IS BEYOND GOD'S REACH

SOMETIME AFTER TURNING TWELVE, THE VIOLENCE ENDED. NO DRAmatic event occurred. It just faded away, never to be spoken of again. Shortly afterward, my dad got a national sales job, and just like that, he was gone from my life, at least emotionally. He traveled the country every week. He came home on weekends. He was all work, all day, every day.

Sometimes on Saturday mornings, my dad would take me to Hardee's for a sausage biscuit. We would sit across from each other in the plastic orange booths, eating in silence.

I was a scrawny kid in middle school. I hadn't yet hit puberty. I wet my bed until seventh grade.

All that was about to change, though. A fire smoldered in the pit of my stomach. A deep resentment and hatred just beneath the surface. All I needed was fuel to set things ablaze. It came in the form of hardcore punk music.

It was a hot summer day in the suburbs of Raleigh, North Carolina. I rode my bike up to North Hills pool. During those long sunny days, the only thing to do was have fun. I thought nothing of riding miles and miles away from home. I spent every day at the pool.

One day, during swim break, some kid was playing hardcore punk music out of his boom box next to the Four Square court. Something awakened inside of me. I no longer felt scrawny, but powerful, like a man. The anger in the music mirrored the anger in my soul fueled by years of injustice and pain.

Like a drill hitting liquid, all the rage and power that was buried under fear, insecurity, and weakness rose out of me. *Black Flag* yelled about rising above. *The Germs* screamed about no God. *The Clash* preached about anger being power. *The Circle Jerks* questioned authority. *Scream* declared we're sick and tired of being rejected; we are fed up. *The Dead Kennedys* declared all religions suck, all religions make me want to vomit.

No more was I the weak boy who wet the bed and rocked himself to sleep. God, authority, teachers, the police, the government, my parents . . . couldn't get to me anymore. I found my tribe, my crew, my brotherhood. Finally feeling untouchable, I was safe.

All through my high school years, I was the front man in several hardcore, crossover speed metal and pre-goth bands. *The Minors, Bloodbath, Second Coming, Blood & Roses.* We gained some local fame, toured around playing shows in bars, house parties, festivals, wherever we could.

Most of my high school years were spent outside my home, hanging at my guitarist's house on Ashe Avenue. The guitarist from *Corrosion of Conformity* lived there and many other "scene" kids. Many were high school dropout intellectuals, hardcore musicians, art school college kids, record store clerks, tattoo artists . . . all living as a tribe of troubadours. Every weekend the place was packed, cranking tunes, writing music, skateboarding, and hanging out. It was my home away from home.

None of this changed the fact that I was on edge most of the time, anxious and still deathly afraid of my father. Drugs helped calm me down a little but also led me into trouble with the law. The police had me for drug possession multiple times, serving plenty of community service hours and one evening in jail.

Somehow, I managed to graduate high school. Shortly afterward, my band kicked me out, got a new singer, released an album, and went on tour. The guitar player was mad because I'd forgotten song lyrics during live performances because I was high.

My band and others in the music scene started to hate me. My reputation was a self-consumed druggy jerk who had no respect for anyone, including himself. It was all catching up to me. I decided it best to get out of town, out of the Raleigh band scene, and go to college at UNC-Wilmington where I heard they had good half pipes and skate parks.

GRADY'S PRAYER

When I arrived at freshman orientation, I ran into Grady, an old friend from the Raleigh band scene. He was a hardcore singer in the band *U.N.I.C.E.F.* (underneath I can't even feel). It had been a while since I had seen him because he became a born-again Christian and left the scene a year earlier.

My former drummer, Sam, from the band *Second Coming*, had all the details about Grady. Sam's parents made him attend church sometimes and on one occasion, Grady gave his testimony there. Sam was furious as Grady spoke of his "old" life compared to his "new" life in Jesus. Sam came back and tore Grady to shreds, destroying any reputation he had in the whole music scene. To us, Grady was a betrayer, giving into everything we hated and stood for. Personally, I always liked him. He was kind and considerate of others in a scene full of egos and backstabbers.

Grady coming to Jesus upset a lot of people, including the band *Corrosion of Conformity* (aka *C.O.C.*). They were the local boys that had breakout fame from the NCHC (North Carolina Hard Core) scene, establishing the crossover-punk-metal genre, touring with *Metallica*, *Iron Maiden*, and getting worldwide attention.

They sang about Grady's "delusional" conversion in the song "Holier," later covered by *Metallica* in their tour sets.

> *"Holier, much holier than you were before*
> *no more*
> *Now your purpose, Jesus, flowing in your soul*
> *No more"*

To me and many others in the scene, God was a cop-out, an escape from reality. An excuse to maintain the status quo. A capitulation to the plastic society that swept the pain we suffered under the rug. Grady had joined the hypocrites.

The reality was, I was one of the biggest hypocrites there. I held in high regard the Straight Edge movement started by Ian McKaye of *Minor Threat* out of the hardcore punk scene in Washington D.C. No drugs, no alcohol, no cheap sex, all to keep the mind sharp in hopes to bring reformation to a broken society. I lived up to none of these ideals while I joined others who also did not live up to those ideals, calling Grady a hypocrite. The joke was on us.

It was a shock to see Grady at UNC-Wilmington. Last I recalled, he was yelling at the audience from the front of his band *U.N.I.C.E.F.*, wearing black eyeliner, his head shaved. Here he was looking like a Jesus lightbulb. Long, blond, curly hair like from an eighties hair band. A smile from ear to ear with sunbeams coming out of his eyes. What the hell had happened to him?

He was so happy to see me, an old friend from our tight-knit scene. I was happy to see him, too, but cautious. As the semester rolled on, it did not take long for him to start talking to me about Jesus. Our conversations went something like this.

GRADY: Jesus is the answer you are looking for.
ME: I'm glad you found what you were looking for, but I'm not looking. I'm good.
GRADY: Would you come with me to a meeting on campus?
ME: No.

He knew my druggy ways were in full swing at university, so he started to pray an outrageous prayer for me, though I didn't find out about it until later. "God, please reveal yourself to Troy in a radical, undeniable way either through his dreams or through drugs."

God was about to answer that prayer.

On a Saturday night in January, during my freshman year, Mark (not his real name), my dorm mate, and I decided we would trip on acid. By all appearances, Mark was an affluent son of a surgeon from Chapel Hill, North Carolina. He was nothing special to look at, a typical clean-cut southern boy. Yet when people drank or did drugs with Mark, they all commented on how he would change. It was so dramatic that he earned the nickname "the Devil." People were afraid of him. He was not what he appeared to be. He had an evil lurking deep in his soul that scared everyone, including me.

During our trip, he seemed to have demonic control or power over me. It was as if he could read my thoughts and control my actions, like something you'd see in a horror movie. Even in my LSD-reality, it seemed too real to ignore. It was all mental and spiritual, with little to no words spoken. The spiritual battle came to a head in the wee hours of the morning.

Mark confronted me one last time, then God showed up unexpectedly. Like a whisper in my head, God spoke to me for the first time. "By affirming the Lord as your Savior, thus upon the Devil will always be defeated, shall always be defeated. The Lord shall always prevail!" The phrase continued, over and over again, gaining volume, clarity, and strength each time. The encounter was silent, no words spoken. The spiritual showdown between good and evil was in slow motion until Mark screamed, cursing God's name, and stormed out of our dorm room. Instantly, my mind was clear and completely sober. God had just revealed Himself to me in an undeniable way.

The next day after class with Grady, I got to share my encounter with him. Tears started to well up in his eyes as he shared what he had been praying for me for months.

It took me seven months to fully surrender to Jesus, but he won me over with the love I felt in that first radical encounter. No more girls, drugs, or Satanic music. No more depression, anxiety, arrogance, sin cravings, and any other hindrances. After I surrendered to His love, I was completely free.

Grady was involved with Cru-campus ministry and introduced me to it. As a new believer, I had a lot to learn. One thing that stuck out was the concept of spending time alone with God, reading the Bible and praying. There was a nature walk on UNCW's campus that provided plenty of seclusion.

Meandering along the nature path, I came across a small clearing in the bend of one of the trails. A private location to sit with my back against a pine tree. One day when I finished praying and reading my Bible, I opened my eyes and there was a robin sitting on a branch in front of me. I smiled and said, "Well, hello Holy Spirit." It became the place where I met God every day until I graduated. Each day when I finished praying, I'd open my eyes and a robin would always be nearby.

BOY MEETS GIRL

Shortly after graduation, my parents gave me a two-month rail ticket through Europe and a flight to Australia for my sister's wedding in Sydney. For an entire year, I was a vagabond. I backpacked and hopped trains through most of Europe and hitchhiked up the Australian east coast from Sydney to Cape Tribulation just below Cooktown in the aboriginal wilderness. I worked odd jobs and at ministries on and off through the year. When the money ran out, I returned to Wilmington. An old friend from the college ministry offered me a job as a substance-abuse counselor at a local outpatient mental health clinic. The Christian community from college migrated to a New Vineyard Church in the area. The Vineyard Church movement was started by John Wimber in the eighties. They emphasized how everybody in the church operated in supernatural gifts. Every Sunday was an adventure as you never knew what would happen.

My life was simple. Get up, go surfing at Wrightsville Beach, go to work late morning, go to church, hang with friends, write songs on my guitar, repeat. That was a snapshot of my life for years. I learned to play acoustic guitar in college and started writing music. I wrote mostly worship and spiritual songs that I shared with my small church community.

Eventually, the pastors asked me to oversee the young adults small-group ministry—sixty of us across five small groups.

That is when the prettiest girl I had ever seen entered into my world. Kathy Casola was stunningly beautiful and six years younger than me. After graduating high school, she joined the young adult ministry. After church, I would get a glimpse of Kathy across the sanctuary and my heart would jump. We ended up in a small Bible study together. All the guys were interested in her. Kathy was beautiful in every sense of the word—physically, in personality, and spiritually. Eventually, I gained the courage to ask her out. She said yes and we started dating.

We had fits and starts across a year and a half of dating, due to my immaturity and my inclination to "over-spiritualize" everything. Is this God's will? This all seems too simple. Is it okay to be attracted to her? Shouldn't there be some large spiritual reason we are together? God, should I marry Kathy? Will You give me a sign?

We were really different, but the one thing we had that has never left us was a strong physical attraction to one another. What a wonderful God-given gift to have a deep, enduring attraction to one another. Kathy was spontaneous, innocent, friendly, and genuinely fun-loving. I was calculating, cynical, socially intimidating, and brooding. We were a funny pair. I learned to laugh and she learned to consider deep thoughts about the nature of man, the universe, and God. I got the better end of the deal.

It became clear to me after dating for a year that I deeply loved Kathy and wanted her as my wife. In the rain, by the oak tree off fourth street in historic downtown Wilmington, I got down on one knee and asked her to marry me. She said yes.

We had a little money from the wedding so we decided to move across the country and start our new life in Portland, Oregon. We both wanted to get out of Wilmington and experience new things. We spontaneously decided to up and move. Portland was so different from North Carolina. Every day was an adventure, but not the good kind.

Kathy discovered as soon as our difficult honeymoon ended that I was a moody, cruel, and unstable person. I flipped a switch days after we married.

What should have been a sexual celebration ended up being a convoluted mess. All my pre-Christian sexual mistakes and insecurities came back to haunt me shortly after our wedding day. Kathy did not know what to make of me. I did not want to have sex hardly at all. I did not talk to her about it. She was hurt and alone through no fault of her own. She just wanted to enjoy our new married life.

An emotionally abusive pattern emerged early in our marriage. It would not be the last time I blamed Kathy or emotionally attacked her for problems that sourced from my own troubled psyche. I regret every one of those dark days that should have been so joyous.

DAD COMES FOR A VISIT

As a husband, I had no clue what I was doing. Shortly after our wedding, my dad decided to come for a visit. He wanted to take me to a Promise Keepers event in Bend, Oregon. Promise Keepers was a large Christian men's movement that held stadium rallies in the nineties all around the United States. Their message championed the fidelity of marriage. Hundreds of thousands of men attended these events.

When he arrived, it was pleasant but a little uncomfortable. We were not used to speaking or interacting a whole lot. I was intrigued about why he came and went along for the ride in hopes something good would come out of it. The event was powerful, infusing into my soul the God-given nobility of manhood.

Then awkward arrived like an uninvited dinner guest. From the stage boomed the speaker, "How many of you came with your dads or sons?" Cheers erupted all over the stadium. "How awesome to come before God as father and sons! Now we are going to do something that I know the sons are going to love. Dads, turn to your sons now. Give them the biggest bear hug of their lives and let them know how much you love them."

My emotional reaction to the speaker's declaration was all over the place. In a flash, I went from resistant and resentful for this forced interaction to a deep longing from the boy within. My heart was crying out.

I was weary from spending my whole life trying to figure everything out on my own. It was exhausting to fail, time and time again, with little sense of how to do it right the next time. If even for one moment I could rest in the strong arms of my father, it would be such a welcomed relief.

Overwhelmed, I went limp and leaned into my father's chest. At twenty-seven, I felt like a boy needing to be held and loved by my dad. Then it happened. He stiffened, clearly uncomfortable with my need for physical affection. He put his rigid arm around me. With his hand, he patted my shoulder three times. Pat, pat, pat. My dad was not ready to do what he came for.

Embarrassed and ashamed of my feelings, my body, too, became rigid. I straightened my back and broke away from his guilty attempts at affection. My surroundings moved in slow motion.

Deep within my soul came the voice of the me as a young boy. "I am alone. I will figure out how to be a husband and family man on my own." From that moment on, I never looked back, diving headlong into one fatherhood faceplant after another.

CHAPTER 3
WAIT, I'M NOT READY TO BE A DAD
GOD FATHERS US AS DADS

I WAS SITTING IN A COFFEE SHOP ON 23RD STREET IN PORTLAND, journaling one early Saturday morning before Kathy woke up. God spoke to me out of the blue while I was drinking a double cappuccino.

"You will have a son in the fourth year of your marriage, and you are to name him David, for he will be a man after My own heart."

In my grand plan, we were not going to have kids for the first five years of our marriage. I came home and told Kathy. She did not know what to think about it. Relieved, I told God I wanted five years without kids, but four would work, thanks. I needed practice time as a husband.

Kathy was on the pill at the time, but it was messing with her hormones big time. The emotional side effects she was having were so detrimental to our relationship, we both decided it was best for our marriage for her to stop taking those "devil" pills. Now we were in the game. We played spin the wheel. Will we or won't we get pregnant today?

Within two months, Kathy was pregnant.

We spent our first year of marriage getting ready for parenthood. Cribs, nurseries, Babies 'R' Us, Lamaze classes at the hospital . . . we were on the fast track to becoming an instant family. We were clear across the country from both of our families. God richly provided a loving church family who came alongside Kathy to help her get ready.

I worked in St. Helens, Oregon, outside the city, as a drug prevention-education specialist at the elementary and middle schools in the district. All the kids who came from drug addict or alcoholic homes would attend group therapy with me during the school day. It was a sad, difficult job, but it paid the rent. Being around troubled kids all day, every day increased my future parenting anxiety. I had a nagging feeling I was going to screw this whole dad thing up.

Kathy and I decided to not find out the gender of our baby beforehand. She had a notion it would be a girl. To add to the fun, she wanted to have a natural childbirth. How very Portland. The beautiful rainy day arrived, and we headed to St. Vincent Hospital to have our very first child.

Kathy was in labor for four hours. By the time she screamed for drugs, she was too far along for the doctor to administer an epidural. She birthed a ten-pound, beautiful baby girl naturally. We named her Kathryn Rayn, which means "pure queen."[1] We call her by her middle name, Rayn. The most remarkable thing happened right after she was born. The doctors handed Rayn to Kathy to hold, and at the first sight of her mommy and daddy, she smiled.

Right then and there, we both knew Rayn was supposed to be with us. No doubts. No second thoughts. It was not too soon; she arrived right on time. All my anxieties melted to nothing as I stared into her beautiful blue eyes. Being a dad is the greatest thing in the world. I was so happy.

A PIT IN MY STOMACH

The thirty-seven-mile commute along Highway 30 from Portland to St. Helens is stunning. I'd pass by the iconic St. John's bridge with its green castle-like spires towering high into the morning sky. I'd follow the Columbia River to the right and the Forest Park mountain range to the left, which included a series of cascading waterfalls. The early morning scene was even more spectacular when the sun rose over the ridge.

---

1. *Kathryn* means "pure" in many languages, including French, Greek, Irish, and Latin. *Rayn* means "queen" in French and English.

On one of these daily commutes in the early summer, when Rayn was seven months old, the Lord spoke to me again out of the blue. "Go to Columbia Biblical Seminary for a one-year program." Since graduating from UNCW with a degree in Social Work, I'd dreamt of either becoming a missionary in a far-off land or going into ministry. But God thwarted my efforts across many attempts to go to Regent University in Virginia Beach, Fuller Theological Seminary in Pasadena, or Gordon Conwell in Boston. Eventually, I gave up and went on with my life. What I heard on my commute that morning was God granting me my heart's desire without me even asking. When I researched the school, it was located in Columbia, South Carolina, close to our parents in North Carolina.

We were broke in those early days. It cost a hundred dollars to apply for school. We prayed that if God wanted us to go, he would have to provide the money to apply. The next day in the mail was a check from the insurance company stating we had overpaid our premium by a hundred and ten dollars months earlier. I applied and was accepted. By the fall, I was enrolled in seminary and graduate school of world missions as God provided miraculously each step of the way.

Rayn was nine months old and as beautiful as ever. I have a vivid memory of her in her car seat in the extended crew cab of our U-Haul as we rode across America, giggling and smiling the whole way. Now that we had Rayn, Kathy was happy to be back on the east coast near her family.

Shortly after arriving in South Carolina, we discovered Kathy was pregnant again. In Portland-hippie fashion, we decided again to not find out the gender of the baby. I pondered the word I had received years before. Would we have a boy?

Just as the Lord had said, we had a boy going into our fourth year of marriage. We named him Avian David. We called him Avi, which is a Hebrew name that means "God is my father." He was my "little buddy" as I used to call him. He was a happy baby.

Having a boy changed me. The weight and reality of passing on healthy masculinity fell hard on my shoulders. Avi was not going to learn to ride a bike alone.

Pressure started to mount on me as a young father. We lived off of financial support from the Vineyard Church in Wilmington, NC and a part-time income from UPS that also included health insurance. The seminary married housing was a trailer park next to campus. We drove a donated car from old Cru ministry friends who supported us during our time in seminary. The school and workload were high, but the financial strain took its toll on my psyche. Our family had to get food stamps in order for us to have enough food to eat and feed Rayn. We were living off of government subsidies. Was I this much of a loser to lead my family here?

My temper started to flair like never before. I'd blow up at Rayn if she did something and at Kathy if she didn't do something. As the pressure continued, the more I overreacted to everyday stresses of family life. On any given day, I was moody or sullen, not sharing with Kathy what I was feeling. She was left to wonder what was going on with me.

The space where I studied in our home was a room only big enough for a desk. When I'd scoot my chair back from it, I'd hit the paneled wall behind me. One day, I was doing some studying on the Old Testament. Rayn, who could not walk yet, was playing with a boom box in the living room. She was toddler. I got up and walked over to her. "Stop touching the boom box, Rayn!" Then I returned to my study.

Being a typical baby, she continued doing what occupied her attention in the moment. She wouldn't stop touching the boom box. At some parenting teaching I received at church back in Portland, I learned never to give a directive twice. The child either obeyed promptly or they were disciplined.

In my frustration with everything that was going on in our life, a flash of anger came over me. Throwing back my chair, I went to physically move her away from the boom box. I yanked her up off the floor by one arm . . . and dislocated her shoulder. She let out a blood-curdling scream. I knew immediately I had seriously injured her. Kathy rushed in from the bedroom to take in the shocking scene, though she hadn't witnessed what happened.

Kathy took Rayn immediately away from me, picked her up, and started rocking her. She tried to comfort her, but nothing was working. I confessed everything right then and there.

A pit of anguish and regret settled into my stomach, a feeling I would become familiar with in the years to come. Tears come to my eyes still as I write about hurting my innocent little Rayn, who I love so much, because of some stupid boom box.

I had physically abused my little girl through harsh punishment and intolerance. The irony was not lost on me. There I was in seminary learning the Hebrew and Greek words for *love* while lashing out in physical anger at my baby Rayn. I was a monster.

Who was going to rescue my family from me? More and more, the cracks started to show in my parenting. I was unstable, unsafe, and afraid of my uncontrollable anger. My stress was uncontainable, and I was taking it out on the ones I loved the most.

I made Kathy take Rayn to the clinic while I said I had to go to work, like a coward. She told the doctor what happened. After she returned, I expected a call from child services, but it never came. Rayn could not crawl for three weeks because she had to wear a sling.

After this incident, my father-in-law threatened me over the phone. I'll be honest, I am grateful he did. He told me if I ever laid a hand on any of his grandkids, he would come after me. He put the fear of God in me. Immediately, we told the family life pastor at the seminary what happened.

The following week, my counseling started with him. Things at home settled back down. No more incidents occurred while I was in seminary. But the damage had been done.

Kathy was leery of me. I sought to make things right all the while being unclear how to change my inner self. My anger, my instability, my isolated nature continued. I continued attending counseling provided by the seminary family life pastor. I don't recall it ever helping.

BUT GOD, I TRUSTED YOU

A year and a half later, I completed my graduate certificate of Biblical Studies. Kathy tried to convince me to stay one more year to get my Masters of Theology or Intercultural Studies. But I believed God had spoken and my relationship with God was not open to input, even from my wife. My isolated and foolish ways continued, to the detriment of my family. I sought multiple ministry positions, then selected one I thought God was leading me to.

Along the way, the seminary president and my professors sought to give me advice, but I ignored them. They suggested I join an established missions ministry I admired, like Samaritan's Purse with Franklin Graham, to learn how nonprofit missions organizations functioned. My in-laws wanted me to consider a youth ministry position, as my brother-in-laws had done. But I was dead set on forging my own way, as I had done all my life, to prove that God was on my side, and I could do it alone. At the end of our time in Columbia, an opportunity opened up for us in Seattle with the Foursquare Church.

They offered Kathy and I an opportunity to spearhead a short-term missions base for the denomination in the city. It sounded promising, so we loaded up all our belongings on an Amtrak train and shipped it across the country. We flew into Portland to see old friends and then headed to Seattle. It was a whirlwind week. The large inner-city Foursquare Church said they would be more than happy to have us, but informed me it was a 100 percent self-funded position. We would need to raise all our monthly support from donors to take on the role. The church was located in a rough part of the city.

My head spun. What had I done? We'd barely made it financially as a family during seminary; how would we survive in Seattle? Immediately, I let Kathy know we were not doing this. She encouraged us to pray about it. No way. God had betrayed me, and I was done with following Him by faith.

We stayed long enough to ship our belongings to Wilmington, where Kathy's parents lived, and followed behind without a penny to our name or a shred of dignity left in me as a father, the leader of our broken-down family.

For the next six months, we lived in Kathy's old bedroom with Avi and Rayn in tow. There was no desire in me to return to social work after having gone to seminary with the intent to go into ministry. I sought associate pastor or missions pastor roles around the country and nothing materialized. I ended up taking a contract job with the state helping to grade reading comprehension tests for the North Carolina school district for eight dollars an hour. I could not even make enough money for us to rent our own place or feed us.

Looking back, it was clear the Lord was providing a stable and loving home for Kathy and the kids at my in-laws' house. Some level of healing and strength was being regained in Kathy's heart by living in a safe environment again.

For me, those were dark days. The abusive history with Rayn, my father-in-law's constant presence as a reminder, and my faceplants greeted me every day. I could not wait to get out.

Kathy has two brothers who had been youth pastors and traveling youth evangelists. Kathy grew up doing ministry with them. Her family, again, encouraged me to consider that route of ministry. I resisted everything her parents tried to do to help me as I thought I had more to offer than just being a youth pastor. My heart was full of pride, as if I had anything to be proud about. God bless their gracious patience; I was no joy to be around.

Resentment grew in my heart toward the Lord. I believed He had led me to this humiliating end intentionally. My interpretation had everything to do with the unhealthy relationship I had with my own father and its impact on my view of God as a loving Father.

After several months, Kathy was done with my arrogant, disrespectful, unthankful, sulking ways. She told me this was the last straw for us as a couple. If I did not change, we were done.

Eventually, I capitulated to family pressure and started to look for youth pastor jobs. I figured someone would hire me with my background as a teenage substance abuse counselor, and it could be a ticket out. They did. We landed a job as youth ministers of West Ridge Christian Church outside of Pittsburgh.

NOT CUT OUT AS A YOUTH PASTOR

Kathy was in her element in the new church because she had years of experience doing youth ministry. What came naturally to her was work for me. Not to be outdone by God's anointing on Kathy's life, I started to push her out of the ministry. God's natural calling and giftings in Kathy created jealousy in me. From that point on, she had to fight to be part of the ministry. This caused tremendous tension between us as I tried to prove I could do this ministry thing without her help. Our senior pastor picked up quickly that something was wrong with me. He mentioned something to Kathy, but she did not divulge how bad I was. No mention of what I was doing to her and our marriage.

He tried to forge a trusting relationship with me, but I did not trust anyone in authority. I kept our relationship at an employee-employer level.

Tensions continued to grow in our marriage, especially as Kathy saw how much I did not have a heart for the current youth ministry. One day she came to me. "Why did you accept this job?" she asked. "We needed money, and we needed to move out of your parents' house." She was disappointed by my motives since it did not reflect her sincere heart for the Lord and His work.

Kathy and I ran a youth coffee shop, arcade, and band venue called Ground Level in the basement of our church. We did many evangelistic concerts and weekly discipleship meetings. We saw a lot of fruit in salvations and a vibrant youth group.

One youth night near the time of my birthday, Kathy dressed up Rayn and Avi in clown makeup and wigs. They came parading downstairs to Ground Level beaming, waiting for their daddy to notice their special outfit for his special birthday. Kathy was just as excited. Insert another fatherhood faceplant. As soon as I saw them, I was dismissive and irritated. I quickly told my kids they were cute, then cut eyes at

Kathy, communicating, *Why did you do this when you know we are starting youth group right now?* It's important to note there were only fifteen kids there that night. Kathy had planned to make my birthday special.

All these years later, I could not tell you anything about that youth group night. But the pangs of regret from dismissing little Rayn, Avi, and my thoughtful wife Kathy, still cut deep. My family was the most important thing happening that night. Fatherhood faceplants hurt everyone involved for years until they are resolved.

Tensions continued to grow between Kathy and me until our pastor recommended I get some help. I started to go to counseling.

In the middle of receiving counseling, my pastor said, "Some people can stay in the ministry while they work through family issues and some cannot." I told him I could not play pastor while my marriage was falling apart. We only stayed on as youth pastors for six more months, making our total time in Pittsburgh fifteen months. Through friends back home, I secured a job as a software testing engineer back in Raleigh.

Upon leaving West Ridge Christian Church, our pastor pulled Kathy aside. He gave his most sincere condolences, acknowledging the pain Kathy was suffering being married to me. He and the pastor's wife felt terrible for her. He told Kathy he clearly saw God's calling on her life for ministry, and thanked her for serving the church wholeheartedly for the time we were there.

He saw in me a troubled husband who was not open to any input or help from anyone. He encouraged her to reach out to him and his wife if she ever needed anything.

So we moved again, making it five moves in three years.

I AM GOING TO FATHER YOU

When Kathy and I got to Raleigh, we attended a church service where there was a prophet. As soon as he saw us, he called us up to the stage out of a crowd of a thousand people. He gave me the following word from the Lord:

"I want you to know, my son, I have brought you here to establish in you the Fatherhood of God and My love for you.

There was a time when the only way you could learn was the hard way. You've hit your head against more walls, bumped into more things, collided with more authority. There was a pain that ripped the heart out of your family. There was time that you were like Jacob. Everyone had to wrestle with you, everyone had to deal with you.

Truth of it is, you were starkly lonely and deeply rejected.

You are filled with talent, filled with might, filled with strength. There is a deep, bold, pioneering edge to you, says the Lord. There was a time when you said, 'I have drunk this cup before and it turned bitter, when you drank of the kingdom.'

I have brought you here not only to establish you in My Fatherhood, but to make you a father. I am going to raise you up, and I am going to use you.

I am not only bringing you here for a season, says the Lord. This is home to you, and I am going to establish you in my Fatherhood. I am going to Father you here. I am going to make up what was lacking in your fathering, says the Lord.

I am going to speak into the most sensitive issues of your life. You have been scared to death you wouldn't be a good father and a good husband. You feel something is going to hound you and pound the two of you. That somehow you wouldn't make it and somehow you would be a betrayer. I want you to know I am breaking that off of you.

I want you to know, says the Lord, there is a unique calling that is over you and your wife to a younger generation. There is a form of calling that has been buried in you like a treasure, says the Lord. I am going to bring it forth and bring it up.

You feel like David who said, 'I've always been battling Sauls.' There have been professional battles, professional loggerheads. You feel like, 'I have had so much trouble getting along with people that are over me.' I want you to know, my son, I am going to deal with some of these issues that come up in you because it has not always been them.

Sometimes you feel like, 'I have too short of a fuse. It is like something is ticking inside of me all the time. I just know, it will only last awhile.' When good times come, something is going to blow up. Your wife crosses her fingers and wonders, 'How long can he make it or take it or do it?'

I want you to know I am coming into that place of pain, and I am coming into that fuse area.

Let me tell you, My son, all your life you have tried to make someone proud. All your life you were going to make them proud. You were going to do it. You were going to earn it.

Let me tell you right now, I am proud to call you My son.

It is not about what you can accomplish or how fast you can run. The great curse of your life was talent. You were always being measured against some form of talent you had, that you had to live up to. My Son Jesus lived up to everything I called for. He lived perfectly so that My unconditional love might pour out and wash over your life right now."

Then he turned to Kathy and spoke this from the Lord:

"My daughter, in this hour, I am coming to you very tenderly. You are one, says the Lord, who lives beyond yourself. You say, 'I am going to be the last person I think about. I am going to love my kids. I am going to love my husband.'

There has been a sense of rootlessness that has troubled you, says the Lord. You say, 'We need to let a certain form of roots down.' I want you to know, you are going to find a haven in this place.

I want you to know there is a unique gift to mother and disciple that I am going to begin to cultivate in you and stir in you. As it stirs, some issues are going to begin to come up. They are not coming back up to torment you, no. But I am going to begin to bring a deeper measure of healing to you.

You know what it is? You feel like someone's eye is always on you. You feel you are under this critical eye, no matter what you do. Like a microscope is always on you. I want you to know, I know everything about you, and I am in love with you, says the Lord.

My love is going to rise up and make this place a haven of healing, health, and blessing. I have put you here, says the Lord."

Our heads were spinning. How could God say these things? After all my faceplants, it made no sense. Kathy was reeling, wondering how this could happen after all I had put her through. I tucked it away and limped forward. He was right about one thing.

I needed to be fathered.

CHAPTER 4
ON THE BRINK OF DEATH
GOD CAN USE TRAGEDY TO TURN YOUR HEARTS TOWARD HOME

ONCE IN RALEIGH, WE STAYED WITH FRIENDS UNTIL WE HAD ENOUGH income to rent a place. Kathy worked the early-morning shift at a local Starbucks. I would get Rayn and Avi ready for the day, singing songs in the bathtub and eating sugary cereal for breakfast. Afterward, I would meet my wife at the coffee shop, drop off the kids, and go into work.

Kathy and I decided not to separate after several months in Raleigh. She asked me to stop seeking ministry opportunities as I had done most of our marriage. I had so many mixed motives around ministry that Kathy saw right through. At the time, I did not see my glaring selfish ambition to be the center of attention, but it polluted any sincerity I had to try and serve God full time. I agreed and turned my focus to surviving in my current job where I had no clue what I was doing. A social worker and pastor by training, how did I end up working as a software testing engineer? I learned on the job like a drowning man gasping for air. It had to work or we were sunk.

Things did not magically get better at home just because we were both busy. Hurt was like an underground river that ran right through the middle of our family. Our church offered an inner healing ministry and retreat called Cleansing Streams. I attended. It brought some clarity and help to me. Like most ignorant men, I thought a few teaching sessions and a weekend retreat was all that I'd need to wipe away years of hurt, dysfunction, and pain. I was wrong.

After Cleansing Streams, life at home continued to be tense. We decided to go to couples counseling with an older couple from our church. It did not go well.

I was charismatic to others but cruel to Kathy behind closed doors. Eventually, the counselors turned against Kathy, blaming her for the turmoil in our home. Kathy refused to go back and rightfully so; the male counselor was as manipulative, cruel, and full of Scripture as I was. This was another nail in the coffin of what felt like a hopeless marriage. The truth was, I was blind to the cruel ways I handled Kathy's heart. I just wanted all the consequences of my actions to be over and demanded she just get with the program. Kathy struggled to trust me, respect me, or show kindness to me—and she had plenty of reasons.

I added another fatherhood faceplant to the growing list. In private, I was cruel in my interactions with Kathy, but in front of the kids, I would treat her nicely. It was classic emotional abuse. The kids would wonder why Mommy was being mean to such a nice daddy. I would turn to her in front of the kids and ask her what was wrong, knowing full well that she was upset over the way I'd just harshly and judgmentally spoken to her behind closed doors. It was evil in its lowest form.

This manipulative pattern played out in front of our kids, pastors, counselors, friends, and anyone else who I could get on my side of our marital issues. Kathy just needed to forgive me for my missteps because isn't that what a good Christian wife should do? The problem with that equation was I continued to sin against her daily in my verbal interaction without remorse or repentance. I used Scripture to back up my position, all the while emotionally abusing her and manipulating my children's emotions against their mother.

It came to a head one day, and Kathy asked me to leave. I honored the request and moved in with a friend for a week or so. The jolt of separation was enough to sober me up to the truth of my abusive ways. Humble and repentant, I returned home.

As a result, I stopped my emotional manipulation for a season. No more unhealthy Christian counseling, no more inner-healing journeys—just work, bills, and cautious marital interactions.

RUSHED TO THE HOSPITAL

By this time, Kathy and I were two ships passing in the night. I would leave early in the morning and return home before dinner. Kathy would leave for a waitressing job as soon as I got home at night, leaving Rayn and Avi with me for their dinner and bedtime.

One night after work, I came home to Avi in a puffy white dress. Rayn loved to play dress-up with Avi, her live doll. Avi loved to play anything with Rayn. I was furious. How could Kathy allow my son to dress like a girl? All my psychology college classes zoomed through my brain. I yelled at Avi to get that dress off. He was completely clueless that he was doing anything wrong. Another fatherhood faceplant. Looking back, I overreacted in aggression and should have been kinder. I should have just told him I did not want him dressing up like a girl, plain and simple. Rayn and Avi were inseparable and best of buds. I reacted strongly every time I came home to Avi in that dress.

During this time, a curious thing started to happen in our home: the beginning of the bed wars. The kids could feel the tension in the house between Kathy and me. Every night, Rayn snuck out of her bed and came into ours to get some comfort for her anxious heart. She was a restless sleeper, kicking us through the night, so we could tell her to go back to her bed. Then Avi would sneak out of his bed and, unbeknownst to us, climb into bed with us. He slept so still, we didn't even know he was there. Sometime during the night, Rayn would return for another attempt to sleep with us. Once the kicking started, they both would get kicked out of our bed. Like a ninja, Avi would return under our covers undetected sometime later in the night. We would awake in the morning to Rayn yelling at us, "Why did Avi get to sleep with you last night?"

This scene replayed a thousand times over a several years period.

I was ignorant that the kids felt the tension in the home. Another fatherhood faceplant. They just wanted to be comforted between us to let their little hearts know everything was going to be all right. The toxic parenting advice we'd been trained in was still in the back of my mind. They made a huge biblical deal about kids *not* sleeping with Mommy and Daddy at night. Because God knows, in biblical times, all the kids had their own tents to sleep in, right? I still get angry thinking about all the crap I swallowed as a parent with that teaching.

I kicked Rayn out every time, while allowing Avi to stay because he was such a quiet sleeper. That favoritism hurt Rayn and did not allow her to experience the comfort her little heart needed. The reality was, her parents could not argue while they slept. All things were as they should be between Mommy and Daddy in the still of the night.

Unbeknownst to me, anytime I would travel for work, the kids would sleep with Kathy, breaking my "rule" of no kids in bed. I was a fool.

After four years, we finally arrived at a normal, non-ministry, non-counseling, paying-the-bills kind of life. Life was stable. We argued less. I exclusively focused my energy at work, trying to learn all I could. We did fun activities with Rayn and Avi. Life was pretty good.

Kathy and I decided to try and have another child. It went so well with our first two, let's have more, right? Looking back, I'm not sure what prompted us to go for another child at the time.

Kathy got pregnant quickly. We told everyone. Rayn and Avi were so excited to be a big brother and sister. Weeks later, Kathy miscarried. We deeply grieved the loss of our baby, surprised by how intense our sadness was.

Some months later, Kathy was pregnant again. Once we passed the point where it looked like all would be well, we told Rayn to save her clothes because she was going to have a little sister. Kathy and I had a sixth sense we would have another daughter one day. We were over surprises. We wanted to find out the baby's gender this time. On the big reveal day, our little family of four was in the ultrasound room, Avi kicking the chair like seconds on a clock.

The nurse returned with the results. "It's a boy!"

Immediately Rayn teared up and ran out of the room to cry in the bathroom. My wife and I, in shock, looked at each other. A boy?

I was overjoyed God had given us another boy. Then I had an overwhelming feeling. Oh no, God was requiring me to be more of a man.

I was struggling as it was with one boy. How would I be able to lead two boys into manhood? If they grew up to be like me, crap! I didn't even know how to fish, load a rifle, fix anything, coach a football team, keep my grass alive, be a good husband, or even be a good person. They were in trouble. I had the sinking feeling. *I don't know if I can do this.*

Olin Troy was born happy. Within the first week of his life, during a baby check-up, the young doctor shared that Olin's head was a funny shape and his skull may be malformed. The doctor went into all the awful details of what could occur to our beautiful baby boy if his skull never fully formed and his brain was exposed. Within days, he was strapped down to the table with a CT scanner swirling around his head. Kathy and I were distraught.

It turned out to be nothing, but the event took a toll on Kathy and me emotionally.

Olin was our cuddle bug; he loved to be held. I would rock him in our rocking chair for hours. He would sit content and peaceful. God was redeeming my connection to my children, having been so harsh with Rayn and Avi for so long under the cloud of poor parenting direction.

Kathy and I never shook the feeling we would one day have a little girl. We decided not to try to have another child, but to be open if it happened. It did. Within eleven months of Olin being born, Kathy was pregnant again. By this time, I was making enough money at the software company that she no longer had to work. A couple months before her due date, we received terrible, unexpected news.

Kathy had cancer.

She had a spot on her back that the doctors determined was melanoma skin cancer. The cancer surgeons said we would wait a month and a half until our baby was born to do surgery as a first step. If it had spread to her lymphatic system, she would have to go through chemotherapy.

We feared the worst. Could our baby be born with cancer?

Kathy ended up having a scheduled C-section. Having been traumatized shortly after Olin's birth, Kathy and I decided after this cancer diagnosis, we could not emotionally handle having any more children. We decided to get her tubes tied during the C-section.

Abrie Elizabeth was born a happy and healthy baby. She finally arrived! Our beautiful brown-eyed baby girl we always knew we'd have. Thankfully, after running tests, they found no signs of cancer or other complications with her.

During the first week home, while nursing the baby, Kathy began to have difficulty breathing. It quickly escalated and she went to the doctor the next morning. The doctor explained that Kathy had blood clots in her lungs from the C-section, and it was life threatening. She went to the ER immediately. They administered blood thinners and monitored her day and night. I was handed our infant daughter and feared for Kathy's life.

The doctors told us if any of the blood clots reached her heart, she would die instantly. For the first time in our marriage, I was a compassionate and attentive husband. She remained in the hospital for ten days. Kathy stayed in the hospital by herself. Her parents came to help with Rayn, Avi, and Olin as we walked through this terrifying time. I got to visit her daily.

God in His mercy gave us this Scripture, "[The righteous] will have no fear of bad news; their hearts are steadfast, trusting in the LORD" (Ps 112:7, NIV). It comforted us as we believed God would see her through this and the pending cancer treatment.

Kathy recovered but was very weak. Within a month, she had surgery to remove the cancer and all associated lymph nodes that could be cancerous. There was the nagging fear that her blood would clot again after this surgery. She was put back on blood thinners and we waited, holding tightly to this Scripture.

A week later, the oncologist returned with good news: the cancer had not spread to her lymph nodes. She would not require chemotherapy.

FOUR, NO MORE

We had four healthy children. Kathy and I clung to each other and our kids like life depended on it. The days of constant arguing, marital tension, and emotional abuse faded to the background for a season.

Rayn was a curious, intelligent, and strikingly beautiful child with distinctive Native American features. She was a serious child, much like me. She was hyper-creative and usually up to something. One day at the mall, she saw acrobats twirling with large pieces of fabric. That night before bed, Kathy walked into her room. She was standing on her loft bed, both arms wrapped in her curtains, on the verge of leaping off for an amazing acrobatic stunt.

She sang and performed songs every night before bed as well, the constant creative performer. I was a harsh, intolerant, and abusive father to her over the first ten years of her life. The smallest infraction would result in severe spankings with a wooden spoon, usually leaving marks. She tried to avoid getting in trouble at all cost. Needlessly to say, she took to lying to avoid her cruel and frightening father.

Occasionally Rayn and I would have fun together. We would dance and joke. But the daddy she knew was volatile, emotionally unsafe, and unstable. In a nano-second I could violently switch from singing kids' songs about God to yelling at her. She grew up tough as nails as she endured the most suffering out of all my children. She dealt with internal anxiety because of my fatherhood faceplants in harsh discipline, instability, and lack of showing love.

Avi was a kind-hearted, relational child. He loved his big sister and they were close. Rayn was always crafting some mischief for them to get into, and he was the one who usually got caught. He had a great sense of humor like Kathy and seemed to always find the fun in every situation.

He was happy to be with me and found me less intimidating. Avi and Kathy had a tight relationship.

He was harshly disciplined as well, but not as much as Rayn endured. He tried to be tough when spanked but would soften eventually. I left fewer marks on his butt as I became convicted that I was too harsh as a dad. I tried to engage with him as a father in an emotionally healthy way because I knew what it was like as a boy to grow up with an angry dad.

Avi got into football at a young age and showed he was tough. I knew nothing of normal sports, having never played on a team in my youth. I felt intimidated as we entered the world of kids' activities where, as a kid, I had always been a loser. Somehow, I ended up being Avi's football coach in the homeschool league. I worked to step it up for his sake, trying to become the dad he needed.

Olin was always on the move. He loved sports, music, and making noise. All boy, all the time. When he was not cuddling with Kathy or me, he ran at full speed. Some of my funniest memories were watching him play football like his big brother in full gear by himself in the back-yard. He played every position on the team. He would first huddle then break, clap and all. Line up at the line of scrimmage. Fade back as the quarterback. Throw the ball to himself as the receiver. Run, dodge, and weave until he was tackled. Sometimes, he would sustain a serious injury and come into the house to let us know he was coming to the bench to get patched up. He'd drink a Gatorade and moments later, return to his make-believe game to score the winning touchdown in the fourth quarter.

Abrie was all baby, all day. But she was also a warrior. She is a stunning girl, with beautiful Italian features like her mom. I'd joke with friends, saying, "You'd better watch out. She will suck you in with her cuteness, then scratch your face." Abrie's favorite thing to do when not sucking her front two fingers was to scream. We had a loud house, and she had to be heard too. She loved "fuzzies," the stuffing found in pillows and toy animals. She would tear holes in these items to retrieve her treasure. Then she'd walk around the house rubbing her fuzzies between her fingers and face while she sucked on her two fingers.

We loved to sarcastically joke around at our house, maybe too much. When she was in second grade, her teacher wrote *Nice job!* on her homework assignment. She turned to my wife and said, "I guess my teacher did not like that paper." Kathy asked her why. "Well, she wrote *Nice Job!*," Abrie said in her most sarcastic voice.

Abrie brings joy and laughter wherever she is.

It was during this season, God pointed me to Malachi 4:6. "He will turn the hearts of fathers to children, and the hearts of children to their fathers" (ISV). I devoured every book I could find on parenting, the masculine journey, and inner healing. God was turning my heart toward home instead of work or ministry.

HOLD IT TENDERLY

During this season, God started to help me gain insight into being a father. In one of those books, I read that if you are having recurring thoughts of a past event, God may be wanting to show you something.

I was starting to relive the traumatic experience I'd had when I was eight years old. Avi happened to be eight at the time, and it must have triggered something in me. The memory was of when my dad beat up my mother in front of me, dragging me deep into the experience, calling her "very bad." It was constantly on my mind . . . on my commute, during my workouts, at church, and at the dinner table . . . It was like a splinter nagging at me.

One day while wrapping up my day at the office, the Lord interrupted me. He asked me a question. "Do you want to know what that is about?" Pondering the question, I walked out of my office, got into my car, and started to drive home. While driving, I replied, "Yes, I would." He told me to pull over. Exiting off the highway, I pulled onto a secluded road and turned off my car, not knowing what to expect. "Get out your journal," the Lord said. It was my normal practice to write down any "word from the Lord" I got in my journal so I could refer to it later. Then He began to speak to me directly. The exchange felt like the one Moses had in Exodus 33:11. "The Lord would speak to Moses face to face, as one speaks to a friend" (NIV).

"I have given the heart of your children into your hands. Hold it tenderly.

This is where the rebellion against authority and hatred for authority wells from. That day your father took your heart in his hands and crushed it.

You've waited all your life to be healed. Like a kid waiting for his dad to come home. But he never did. Your anger stems from this pain.

This is your wounded place. But I am here to heal it.

I am calling you into fatherhood. A deeper level of fatherhood.

I am placing an anointing on you to father nations."

As the Lord spoke, I was writing and weeping uncontrollably. Ugly tears, snot running down my face, eyes swollen. Suddenly, on my driver's side window, I heard, *BANG, BANG, BANG!* I looked up and saw a large angry man standing outside my car. "What are you doing here?" he bellowed. "You need to move along." Apparently, my car was parked in front of his property. His house was set back from the road. So much for pulling off on a secluded road.

What mercy God had to show me where all this anger was coming from. And then to give me a chance to redeem some of my fatherhood faceplants. I didn't know at the time the process God would use to bring about that healing.

During this time, God gave me dreams and visions about each one of my children. What God thought of them and how He had uniquely made them to bring some element of His glory to the earth. I called it "finding God's thumbprint on my children."

It started with Rayn.

I saw a door partially cracked with a beautiful young woman dressed like a queen stepping into the king's court. It was Queen Esther. Rayn was outwardly beautiful in every sense of the word, like Esther, but what made Esther even more beautiful was her bravery in the face of death to save her Jewish people from the king's wicked assistant. Her inner beauty was what God was showing me in Rayn's character.

With colored pencil, I drew her the vision I'd had, framed it, and gave it to her. God was helping me replace my harsh ways with kindness.

Avi was next. Around this time, there was a great tsunami in Indonesia that killed thousands and thousands of people. Listening to the radio about the great tragedy, there was an amazing story about a pastor who saved his entire church from certain death. While the tsunami sirens sounded, the Lord told him to get his few church members into one of the fishing boats that lined the coast, then to take the small boat and go directly toward the tsunami out to sea. The pastor obeyed, even though it sounded like a death mission.

He ended up saving the lives of everyone on the boat because of his bravery, selfless obedience, and leadership. Immediately, I had a vision of Avi on that boat, the pastor kneeling alongside his congregation as the wind and waves raged around them. Jesus was in the boat, standing with one hand on Avi's bowed head and the other hand outstretched toward a huge incoming tsunami wave, miraculously staying it back.

I drew the vision with colored pencil, framed it, and gave it to him with the following Bible verse: "The people who know their God shall be strong, and carry out great exploits" (Dan 11:32, NKJV).

Next was Olin. I saw him as a young lion walking next to a larger, yet gentle, lion. The larger lion was Jesus. They were in a beautiful African safari scene. Jesus was walking and showing him the way of the pride. I drew this vision in colored pencil and wrote the following Bible verse: "Even youths grow tired and weary, and young men stumble and fall; but those who hope in the LORD will renew their strength. They will soar on wings like eagles; they will run and not grow weary, they will walk and not be faint" (Isa 40:30–31, NIV).

Last was Abrie. I had a vision of a dark night just after twilight. You could still make out the outlines of the blades of grass and plants in a field. The sky was full of lightning bugs like stars in the sky. She was to brighten even the darkest places. As a result, I nicknamed her "lightning bug."

It was an amazing time for me as a father, and I felt the nearness of God helping me step by step. In a worship service at church, I remember pouring out my heart. *God, if I could only but place my children's hands into Your hands, then they will be okay. As a dad, help me. You've done nothing but help me in my life. You will do the same for them.*

Weeks later, I took Rayn and Avi to an event called "The Call" at the Titans football stadium in Nashville, Tennessee. Kathy was a little concerned with my renewed spiritual activity in light of my patchy history with God. But she was supportive and let me take the kids ten hours from home. The Call was a twelve-hour prayer and fasting event just to seek the face of God. Forty thousand people attended the one-day event.

During the event, the Lord laid it heavy on my heart, that I needed to tell Rayn, who was now eleven, about abusing her as a toddler. For two hours, the Lord pressed on me like an anvil from heaven. This would either go well, healing open wounds she did not even know existed, or leave yet another traumatic scar. The impression I got was that until the truth came out, this would remain an open wound the enemy would exploit later in her life.

When I could resist the urge no longer, through gut-wrenching tears, I confessed the horrific scene to her. Repentant and sorrowful, I told her what I'd done and asked her forgiveness. She had no memory of the event and was uneasy. After some time, we embraced and the wound closed. Later in the day, during some of the extended worship sets, we went down to the floor of the football stadium where people were dancing.

Again, the Lord spoke to me. "Tell her, 'I like it when you dance before me.'" Shortly after sharing this with her, she began to praise the Lord in dance like never before. It was a pivotal moment, as years later, dancing became one of her primary ministry giftings. Many have responded to God just seeing her dance.

We made our way back up to the stadium bleachers as the day continued. I looked over at Avi, who was holding his right hand up about shoulder height. He was not praising or worshiping but just holding his right hand open with a big fat grin on his face. I asked him what he was doing. He turned to me and said, "I'm holding Jesus' hand." What?! He went on to describe a detailed vision of Jesus walking up and standing next to him. Avi reached up and held his hand. Jesus and Avi chatted, interacted, and basically just hung out for about thirty minutes, with me noticing just before the vision was over.

I was undone.

CHAPTER 5
THE BEGINNING OF THE END
GOD'S JUSTICE IS HIS MERCY

"IYESUSI GETA NEWI, IYESUSI GETA NEWI!" I BELTED OUT FROM THE front of the Ethiopian Emmanuel church in Addis Abba, Ethiopia. It meant "Jesus is Lord" in Amharic, a principal language of Ethiopia. God had called me there to give a prophetic word to a young indigenous church movement comprised of three hundred or more churches across Ethiopia.

Eddie, a dear friend from UNC-Wilmington, had become a missionary and pastor within the Ethiopian Emmanuel movement. He was a good ol' boy from North Carolina and the only white guy involved in the entire denomination. It was a sovereign act of God how Eddie got involved in one the faster growing indigenous church movements on the continent of Africa.

After my failed attempt at ministry and family, I agreed with Kathy to stop pursuing ministry. Yet I could not shake the desire. It lingered in the back of my mind for years. God was pouring out miracles, salvations, healings, and more through Eddie in Ethiopia, and it stirred my imagination. We had kept in touch since UNC-Wilmington, and what was happening in his life was nothing short of a miracle.

After Abrie's birth and Kathy's dramatic medical scares, it appeared we were finally heading in the right direction. I started to stabilize and so did our home life. My income continued to rise. We had turned a corner and even started to have fun as a family.

Going to Ethiopia would be the first time in seven years that I had done anything related to ministry other than helping with the children's ministry at our church.

Days before I left, God began to show me similarities between the indigenous church movement history and the life story of King Hezekiah. The short of it was as God called King Hezekiah to "get his house in order" by turning his heart toward his children (2 Kings 20:1), so was he calling Ethiopia Emmanuel to turn their ministry focus to the next generation. There were no plans for me to preach while I was in Ethiopia. When the leaders heard the message God had given me, they invited me to give it at the main mother church for the movement. I was bringing the heart of the Father to the people, calling them to go against their cultural norms and pour into the next generation of ministries, fathering and mentoring junior ministers to plant churches and take the movement even further. Culturally, youth and young adult ministries were not a focus for churches in Ethiopia. Their typical approach would be to hold bigger and bigger meetings with seasoned leaders versus discipling the next generation, releasing them into their callings. That ministry approach would result in smaller gatherings lead by younger more inexperienced ministers. This was not the culture of Ethiopian churches as that time, based on my limited experience.

The entire trip was a powerful encounter for me personally. God was not done with me, like I had assumed, because of my fatherhood faceplants. Unfortunately, what I interpreted as the beginning of a calling from the Lord to fulfill my dreams of missions, ministry, and preaching was in fact the beginning of the end.

I started a 501c3 nonprofit organization in hopes to get more international ministry opportunities. Quickly, my focus was pulled away from family and set on my ministry aspirations, which in hindsight were all self-serving and driven by a brokenness. A mixture of arrogance and ambition reared its ugly head again, as it had seven years prior when I thought I was better than "just" being a youth pastor and pushed Kathy out of the youth ministry because of my jealousy.

Kathy continued to serve in the children's ministry at our church. The church recognized the calling on Kathy's life and invited her on staff to become the children's director. She accepted.

As I sought to build my mission organization, she served and loved the children at our local church. Everything Kathy touched, God blessed. She had favor with everyone at church. People recognized the gifting and calling on her life as it was obvious to all. I started to get jealous just like I had when we were youth pastors. While she prospered, I got no traction or support.

From the beginning of our marriage, the emphasis had always been on my calling, my ministry, and my dreams. Kathy could come along, but there was never room for what God had called her to do or us to do together. It was all about me.

I began to pressure her to leave her role at the church to help me build my make-believe missions organization. God was in the process of strengthening and rebuilding her calling that I had torn down over the course of our entire marriage. She declined my generous offer to jump on board a ministry God was clearly not blessing.

In hindsight, I see the call to Ethiopia was a gracious one-off from the Lord. It was not a commission from God to build an entire missions ministry that would one day save me from my boring tech job.

Every Sunday, I had to humble myself and serve Kathy's calling. Kids were getting saved and awakened to their God-given design. Rayn and Avi were deeply involved in the ministry and loving every minute of it. But my emotional abuse reared its ugly head again. As her ministry continued to flourish, I began to emotionally sabotage my wife.

If we were not at the church so much, we could spend more time together as a family. I complained she was gone and otherwise occupied with church life. Putting roadblocks in front of her every decision, my obstinance grew. Sundays went from fun times to a marital battleground.

She eventually reached a point when she'd simply had enough.

Insert another faceplant, not honoring or respecting Kathy's gifting. Turning what should have been a blessing for my children, and other children, into World War III behind closed doors. Even though this was a marital failure, this had a direct impact on my children, as they loved being a part of Mommy's ministry. My behavior toward Kathy robbed them of what God was doing through my wife.

MARRIAGE COUNSELING FAILS

"You want me to quit? Fine, I'll quit," Kathy finally capitulated. Surprising everyone at church and our kids, she resigned. Rayn and Avi were stunned. It made no sense to them or anyone else. Everyone asked why, but she never divulged my abusive campaign against her success because of my jealousy except to her closest friends. The pastor and his wife pulled her aside as other pastors had done, expressing their deep condolences to her and concern for me. Nothing was left but deep hurt. At times, she could not bring herself to attend church.

When she missed, I'd railed against her, accusing her of being a bad example to our kids by not attending church, while my emotional abuse continued. We ended up in couples Christian counseling shortly thereafter.

The counselor was not prepared for my manipulative and hyper-spiritual ways. I had a long list of "God said this" and "God said that" encounters that revealed how my wife was wrong and off in her understanding of our current circumstances. I was out of my mind, leveraging the God card to force Kathy into doing what I wanted. I was not hearing God at all, but the voice of the enemy or my own sinful, tainted perspective. I was breaking every Scripture about loving your wife, all the while thinking I was hearing from God and justifying my cruelty. No one could talk to me. No one could correct me.

Needless to say, no progress was made after five months in therapy. Our counselor recommended we get separated for two weeks before Christmas, just to give Kathy relief from my barrage of verbal and emotional abuse. I continued to blame her for my ministry's lack of success because she would not "support" me.

After the two-week separation, we came back together and things got even worse. I was toxic. She was not going down with this ship this time. I was unrelenting, trying to pin the blame on her for our relationship problems and my unhappiness in life. I see now that God had been resisting me for years because of my arrogance and my treatment of Kathy, but I was blind to it. He would have mercy on me for short seasons. I'd take His blessing as a carte blanche endorsement of my "grand" calling that Kathy just never could get on board with. Truth was, I was full of blind ambition masked in spiritual language and a hell of a lot of brokenness.

Every other day I'd fill five or six journal pages of what I thought God was directly speaking to me, about Kathy, about myself and my amazing calling, about the church, etc. . . . I was starting to lose it. I thought God was "speaking" lies to me about Kathy! I was greatly deceived.

I pulled Olin into my spiritual craziness as I would talk to him about how God was speaking to me about releasing the "Spirit of the Wild." I filled his mind with all kinds of unhealthy and unbalanced views of hearing God's voice while I continued my emotional abuse of Kathy. "God could call you, Olin, out into the wild, and if He calls you, you need to follow His voice."

Thankfully, Olin, at age six, shared what his dad was telling him with Kathy's parents. He said, "Even if Mom tells me to come home, I would not have to obey because God could call me out into the wilderness behind our house, so I could stay there." If a house could ever be filled with demons, our house was. Kathy was horrified. Insert another fatherhood faceplant.

After ten months of couples therapy, our counselor gave up. Refusing to listen or change, I was emotionally swinging at everyone and everything that got near me. It was dangerous for my family, and it was about to get worse.

A SUMMER OF TERROR

In the midst of tearing my family apart with my own hands, along came calling a familiar sin of my youth. Pornography. God gave me victory over this area of my life in my twenties and it had not resurfaced in fourteen years of marriage. During this season, I fell back into the secret sin of my past.

Kathy started to suspect something was going on and confronted me about it. I lied. She confronted me again. I lied. But God showed her I was lying. She confronted me a last time, and I confessed my sin to her. Insert yet another fatherhood faceplant.

Heartbroken and grief stricken, she could take no more. She had had enough of this crazy ride as the wife of Troy Mangum. Nothing but fifteen years of verbal abuse, emotional abuse, hurt, spiritual craziness, and pain. "Get Out! Get Out!" she screamed. "I want a separation!"

Digging in, I told her I was not going anywhere. If she wanted to leave, she could, but she'd have to leave the kids. So began the summer of terror.

She asked me to sleep on the couch. I refused. Kathy slept on the downstairs couch all summer. Every day she woke up in physical pain. I couldn't care less; if she wanted to be comfortable, she could just sleep in bed with me. To get some relief, she stayed out of town or with friends as much as possible, always with the children.

I garnered support from friends, brothers, and other family for my "Christian" position of no separation, using my skills in persuasive and scriptural knowledge. If war was what she wanted, then war was what she would get.

Before the counselor gave up on us, he advised Kathy to tread carefully as "Troy is a ticking time bomb. Troy is dangerous and could turn physically violent if you try and leave." Deeply deceived, I was dead set to make life a living hell for Kathy until she saw things my way.

She was at a prayer meeting at some point during the summer, and a prophetic lady saw her in a vision. Kathy was bent over in a chair with her hands over her ears, rocking back and forth in distress. Her hair was disheveled and tangled. A tornado was raging around her, destroying everything in its path. Pieces of furniture, stuffed animals, and debris caught up in the swirl. All the while, Kathy rocked back and forth, screaming, making a sound no one could hear.

As the arguing continued that summer, she would plead with me, "just *hit* me so the others can see what you are really like." Too cruel and deceptive for that, the verbal tongue lashing and emotional manipulation continued privately where no one would know. Meanwhile, I was kind and lavishing the kids with time, attention, and gifts. They would ask, "What's wrong with Mom?" and I would reply, "I don't know." Another fatherhood faceplant.

As summer drew to a close, it was clear there would be no winners in this detente. I agreed to move out.

GETTING
BACK UP

CHAPTER 6

STOP HITTING YOURSELF

ACCEPTING GOD'S UNCONDITIONAL LOVE

NOT A HAPPY ANNIVERSARY

I remember the day in slow motion.

It was our fifteenth wedding anniversary. It had been two months since I'd moved out. I woke up in my sparsely furnished apartment with a question. Would I reach out to Kathy today and wish her a happy anniversary? I had a tinge of regret for how I had treated her through the summer.

Prior to separating, we returned to our marriage counselor to negotiate the terms of our separation and the rules of engagement.

Our counselor advised Kathy to limit her interactions with me to only what was necessary because of the emotionally manipulative patterns he'd witnessed. As a result, she would not talk to me over the phone, over text, over email, or in person. We only spoke when exchanging kids during visitations.

We did not discuss our separation or possible divorce without our counselor as a third-party witness. If there was anything we needed to discuss, we would meet with the counselor to record and document our interaction. I did not honor our agreement and continued to push. What came next was a sign of how disconnected I was from the reality of our separation.

While still in bed, I texted her, "Happy anniversary" and added something romantic. It was awkward. I hoped to get a reply. I have a vivid recollection of that morning: the shower was lukewarm, the coffee watered down, and the day drizzled rain. I barely got myself together and went into work.

Upon arrival, my boss called me into his office. When I stepped in, the director of HR was waiting for me. There is a white sheet of paper on the table. We were about to have a "crucial conversation."

Over the ten years since we moved to Raleigh, my career continued to grow. By this time, I managed a software engineering team of twenty-five in the U.S. and India for a major tech company. In the last year, while my personal life was unraveling, so was my career. I had lost five employees, the most recent announcing on their way out, "Troy does not know how to manage people."

In my mental and emotional fog a few weeks earlier, I had emailed confidential employee performance ratings and year-end reviews to 300 or more employees at my local office by accident. I exposed the most confidential information between a manager and their employee to everyone.

As I stepped into the office, I took a deep breath. They proceeded to tell me how the leadership team strongly considered firing me because the organization had lost two of their top software engineers under my poor leadership skills. After debating, they decided to strip me of my management title and take away my entire organization as a disciplinary action for my recent missteps.

They slid the paper across the table for me to sign. My job would be to work on special projects as deemed necessary by my senior director. With the stroke of a pen, I was sidelined and my promising career as a leader was over.

It all caught up to me just like it had when I'd been kicked out of the band. The respect my work title garnered meant everything to me; now there was nothing left.

By this time, my nonprofit mission organization had failed. Church leadership knew I had forced Kathy out of her children's pastor position because of jealousy. There was nowhere for me to go.

God was dismantling my world, and all the things I relied on, one piece at a time.

After work that day, I drove home, chain-smoking and on the verge of tears. I turned the key to my apartment and was met with dead silence.

Going over to my couch, I picked up my guitar and wrote:

"It does not make sense that I should rejoice in trials and pain

That there is something that You're doing of eternal gain.

How can you use a broken man?

Why would you use a broken man?

I can't say that I understand

This is a song of a broken man."

I put down the guitar and looked at my phone. She never texted back.

HOW CAN YOU LOVE A COUCH POTATO?

I sat for what seemed like hours in silence with my guitar in hand. Just sitting and staring.

All of a sudden, God's voice broke through. In the back of my mind, I heard "I love you." Ignoring it, I heard it again a little louder and closer, "I love you." His voice moved to the foreground of my conscious mind and shouted, *"I love you!"*

After a moment, I looked up to the ceiling and asked, "How could You love me? I can do nothing for You."

And there it was.

The lie, the vow, the false belief I'd held all my life.

If I was not useful to God, He would cast me aside. If I was not "productive" as a Christian, He would have no use for me. If God did not get a return on His investment, He would move on, leaving me to learn to ride my bike alone.

I tried so hard to be an on-fire and productive believer. I evangelized, read my Bible, had quiet times, fasted, prayed, sought to discern and follow God's will. Now look at me.

A man in the middle of an ash heap called his life.

Even if I wanted to drum up some enthusiasm about God, I could not. All around me were burned bridges and rejection by my own doing. It did not make sense God would love such a useless person as me. Clearly, I was broken beyond repair, otherwise following these "God activities" would have fixed me by now.

I had spent my life responding to God's love with excessive religious activity, while my inner belief system was broken at its core. Conditional love permeated my life before and after I was a Christian.

As much as I did not want my upbringing to affect me, it had. My core beliefs about myself and the world were formed long before Jesus rescued me in college. Excessive "Christian" activity or ministry did not change my deep-seated belief system. They were formed in my crazy and scary childhood. Until Jesus broke through, I remained oblivious to this reasoning.

Growing up, I was very aware at every stage of my life that my parents wanted things from me. Don't tell anyone. Don't upset your dad. Don't be a wimp. Make us look good. Do things we can brag to others about. Don't embarrass us. Don't expose us. Be a leader. Accomplish great things. Look the part.

I felt they did not love me. I was just another damn thing they had to deal with in their stressful, "trying to keep their head above water" lives. It was not true, but it was true to me.

Neither of them ever took any time to get to know me, the real me. The only time I felt love was when their attention turned toward me after some notable accomplishment. Something they could brag to their friends about. You know my son . . . blah, blah, blah.

I never knew love without strings attached. Love just for existing, just because I was their son. No accomplishments, no accolades, no quid pro quo, no nothing—never loved for just being me.

How could God be any different? He wanted things from me, too, right?

My belief about God's love was based on my experience with human love, particularly the love I received from my parents. The Bible says God is a father, so I figured he must be like *my* father.

The Christian circles I ran in emphasized getting busy for God instead of establishing your identity as a beloved child of God. It strengthened the lie that we must perform or show results to be loved. I now know that God's love is not like that.

When I could do nothing "for" God is when His love finally reached my heart. Unbeknownst to me, all my "Christian" activity had kept God's love at a quid pro quo level. He does this for me, I do this for Him. But on that day, sitting in the silence, holding my guitar, His unconditional love and my broken heart collided. At my lowest point, with nothing to offer to God, I finally understood. God loved me first. God loved me most. He loved me because I was His son. Period.

My fifteenth anniversary was the best and worst day of my life.

CHAPTER 7

A LITERAL SIGN FROM GOD

THE GREATEST THING A FATHER CAN DO FOR HIS CHILDREN IS TO LOVE THEIR MOTHER

THE DAYS DID NOT GET SHORTER; THEY GOT LONGER.
The revelation of God's love was like a life ring I held on to while adrift at sea.

On any given day, you could find me chain-smoking cigarettes on my tiny balcony, listening to Sufan Stevens, on the brink of tears. I'd pick up my guitar, write another sad song, and eventually make it to my unmade bed.

Weeks turned into months with no hope of reconciliation in sight.

One day while grocery shopping with Olin and Abrie, I stopped to pick out an item. Abrie said out of the blue, "Even though you left us, Mommy still loves you and so do we." I broke down sobbing in the canned food aisle, my kids staring at me with their innocent faces. Abrie's little hand came over and patted my leg. "It's okay, Daddy."

GOD IS NOT VERBOSE

The one thing that grounded me in my empty apartment was the Bible. Like a drowning man, every morning I reached for it to keep my head above water another day.

One morning, God spoke loud and clear right before I opened the Bible. He said one word, "Elkanah." What the heck was that?

I had never heard that word in my life. It must be a Bible word, so I googled it. There was a reference to the word in 1 Samuel chapters 1 and 2. Elkanah was the husband of Hannah, who was the mother of Samuel. Seems innocuous, but God was about to gut-punch me, in the most loving way of course.

Put on your Sunday school pants, it is about to get flannel graph up in here. Here is a paraphrased version of the story.

Elkanah loved his wife Hannah. Hannah could not bear any children, so she was super sad. Elkanah was dumb enough to marry two wives and his other wife bore him children. The other wife taunted Hannah about not having kids. Sounds awful on multiple fronts.

They all went to Jerusalem like one big happy family to do Jewish things, like go to the temple. While there, Hannah poured her broken heart out to the Lord about not having kids.

Then a priest (Jewish pastor guy) added insult to injury. He accused Hannah of being drunk and told her to get out of his workspace (i.e. the temple). She pleaded with him to hear her out. She shared her plight and sorrows. She declared she would dedicate her son to the Lord's work, if God would give her a son.

The priest prophesied that she would have a son by this time next year, and that is exactly what happened. Samuel was born. But wait, it does not end there.

Hannah was stoked but still had a twinge of sadness. She had a son, but according to the promise she made to God, she had to literally give Samuel to this priest to permanently live and grow up in the temple after he was weaned. Hannah gave Samuel over to the priest when he was around five or six years old.

Because she lived a long way from the temple, she visited her son once a year. God put a special call on Samuel's life at age of eleven. He eventually became the top God guy for the entire Jewish nation and advised King Saul (Israel's first king). God used Samuel to find and appoint King David (Israel's best king who wrote the Psalms) when he was just a teenager. In summary, Samuel was an important dude in the Bible, big time.

What does any of this have to do with me? After I read the Bible story in my quiet apartment, God started to ask me questions.

"Did Elkanah honor his wife's commitment to Me?"

Yes.

"What made Elkanah look past the circumstances to honor his wife's commitment to Me?"

His love for her.

Then He said, "Am I a God who is blind? Yet, you treat me as unable to act on your behalf. I am able, but am I willing? I am the Lord. I raise one up. I lower another down. Are you God that you should choose? I am sovereign! I am the Lord of your wife. Elkanah honored my way with Hannah. He did not interfere.

"Humble yourself under My mighty hand, and I will lift you up. Hannah's sacrifice was Elkanah's sacrifice. It started with my work with Hannah, not Elkanah. I am the Lord. I do not meet your standards or your understanding. You have been arrogant to think I would start with you. I am the Lord who is sovereign and reigns over you and your home. Humble yourself as Elkanah did. Humble yourself and walk in fear before Me. Then and only then will I lift you up. The lesson of Elkanah is the lesson of humility fueled by love for his wife and faithful devotion to Me."

For all of my marriage, I firmly believed God would talk to me first and foremost, as the husband and father, about what He was doing with my family. This was not the pattern seen with Elkanah and Hannah. When we separated, I was convinced I held the correct perspective and that Kathy was clearly in the wrong.

Repenting of my spiritual arrogance opened me up to see things from a different perspective.

THE MOST IMPORTANT THING A DAD CAN DO

Around this time, I attended a men's prayer breakfast at my church. At the end of the event, they asked if anyone needed prayer. I stood up and mumbled something about being separated. Then a gentleman in his seventies stood up to share a story. I will call him Walter to keep his privacy.

He and his wife had been happily married for over fifty years. He shared how they were in the gift shop over thirty years ago and saw a small wall sign. The plaque had dark wooden paneling like a trailer home wall trying to be fancy. The lettering was gold and shaped like something from the sixties version of *Willy Wonka and the Chocolate Factory*. Walter said he was drawn to it and ended up buying it.

They hung the plaque in a prominent place in their home for over thirty years. It was a treasure to their marriage.

The morning of the men's breakfast, the wife sensed from God they were to take it off their wall and give it to someone that day. So he tucked it in his pocket and went to the prayer breakfast in anticipation of what God would do.

Walter welled up with tears in his eyes and turned to me. In front of sixty men, he handed me the sign and said, "This is for you."

I looked down at the words on the plaque through my tears.

It read: The greatest thing a father can do for his children is to love their mother.

God sent a sign, a literal sign.

CHAPTER 8

TRUST BIG, GO LOW

HUMILITY COMES BEFORE HONOR

THE WEEKS CONTINUED TO ROLL ON WITH NO HOPE OF RECONCILIATION. As the harsh reality set in, so did a deep sense of anger and resentment in my heart. Feeling justified and "in the right," I looked for any opportunities to convince Kathy how wrong she was. She was not falling into these manipulative traps any longer.

I kept the sign from God at my work desk as a daily reminder. A convicting reminder. I broke its instructions at every turn with Kathy.

As things looked bleak, I sought counsel from other men. Most of them gave me counsel to move on with my life, because it was clear she was not interested in reconciliation.

One older man, Seth Barnes, gave me counsel that was simple and profound. He had seen many Christian divorces through the years in his time running Adventures in Missions (AIM), all of them sticky situations with irreconcilable differences cited as the reason for the split. In most cases, he saw men kick against humility like their masculine soul depended on it.

His advice to me was, "Trust big, go low." Trust God radically and always, *always* take the position of humility. His advice sounded dangerous to me. It would be a while before I put it to the test.

After seven months, Olin and I were up early one Saturday morning at my apartment. He asked, "Daddy, why do you still wear your ring?" I told him it was a promise I made to Mommy. He said, "Mommy still loves you; she wears her ring. Not all the time, but sometimes. God still loves you too." I had no words.

Days prior to this interaction with Olin, I came under deep conviction like only the Holy Spirit could bring. It came during one of my daily quiet times.

In a moment, God revealed my insolence, arrogance, pride, mean spirit, vengeful, jealous, envious, violent, controlling, manipulating, and deceiving heart. Everything came into clear view. An obscure little verse in the Bible provided clarity to the confusing mess of how and why we were separated.

"We acknowledge our iniquities . . . uttering lies our hearts have conceived" (Isa 59:12b, 13b, NIV).

I had constructed a false perception of why we were separated, justifying all of my behaviors and heart attitudes because I believed God was on my side. Surely Kathy was the one who needed to change and just "let it go." The reality was, I never stopped my abusive and cruel ways of speaking or behaving toward her, all the while demanding she "forgive and forget." My thinking was warped, and I did not see it until my darkness was brought into the light.

When reality sunk in that God was not on my side, and I had been wrong for years without knowing it, I wept on and off, under the conviction of the Holy Spirit, for ten days. My heart had been softened and broken open in the best way possible.

Call me stupid, but I just could not see what others saw about myself until that day. No amount of counseling, mentoring, or other input could bring this level of conviction that only the Holy Spirit can bring. I was seeing clearly from His perspective, what He saw in my heart.

"The Lord is the witness between you and the wife of your youth" (Mal 2:14, NIV).

All of a sudden, Seth's words came to mind. The way home was to trust big and go low. From that point on, I stopped fantasizing about getting a lawyer to defend my case and my cause. I relinquished everything and surrendered to God.

BIPOLAR AND OTHER FUN TOPICS

For years, Kathy had asked that I get a psychiatric evaluation. I refused to go. One time, to prove I was not mentally ill, I agreed to go. I walked out of the psych's office without a diagnosis that required pills. It was such a victory in my mind. I told her, "Never ask me to go again." It was one of many bones of contention between us.

While I was still under the conviction of God during those ten days, I told Kathy what happened. She did not believe it. I had a long list of "spiritual epiphanies" over the years that never changed my behavior or attitudes of my heart toward her.

To prove I was not lying or acting deceptively, I told her I would go to a psychiatrist for an evaluation as she had asked me to do for years. Whatever the doctor recommended, I would follow through on. I was sincere but never expected to come out with a diagnosis.

My dad was bipolar. I hated growing up with a medicated dad. To me, he lived behind glass. There was always a disconnect. He lived in a make-believe, medicated world where everything was fine while I drowned right in front of him.

While in seminary, I wrote papers on how biblical counseling (nouthetic counseling) was superior to the pill-fix culture we lived in. The "bible" of diagnosing mental disorders in secular psychiatry is *The Diagnostic and Statistical Manual of Mental Disorders* (DSM). The diagnoses found in the DSM used alternate words for the sins described in the Bible. I was dead-set against traditional psychiatry. I had a university degree in social work. I understood how antipsychotic drugs simulated and mimicked the body's natural chemicals.

I did not want to become medicated like my dad. That is why I fought my wife for years on this topic. I did not want to join the ranks of the medicated mentally ill where I would be cut off from the real world and living in some "pseudo make-believe everything is fine" world.

I was about to learn what it meant to go lower than I could possibly imagine.

I remember the day the psychiatrist gave me the DSM-IV diagnosis of bipolar modal 2 (bipolar II). I walked out of her office, having lost the last shred of male self-respect I had left in the world. I had become my dad. I joined the ranks of the medicated mentally ill. I had become the person I said I would never be.

I sat in the doctor's parking lot with my friend's words echoing in my head, *Trust big, go low.* I could not imagine a lower place than right there. I chose to put my head in that yoke called mental illness because I had been wrong about everything else. I guess I had been wrong about this too.

It nearly killed me.

I was now at my lowest. I could not look at myself in the mirror. I labeled myself as someone who no longer had the ability to control himself unless he swallowed pills. My pride was crushed in the dust. The only thing I needed now was for drool to come out of my mouth to accompany my shattered catatonic self-image. I could not imagine a lower state.

I held no hope of reconciling with my wife. After I told her my diagnosis, she was relieved but not impressed. She asked, "What are you going to do now?"

I thought to myself, *What am I trying to prove?* Taking pills was not going to help my chances of getting back together with Kathy, so why put myself through such humiliation and self-abasement? Would I actually follow through with what I said I would do?

I had a choice.

Would I walk down the medicated road, something I said I would never do?

Kathy made it clear in our last conversation that this decision was mine alone to make. If I took the medication, it would not affect her desire to be with me or improve our chances of reconciliation. It was like a gunfight at the O.K. Corral in my soul.

Would I die fighting or surrender and possibly live?

I thought, *If God has shown me that my heart had conceived lies around the reasons for our family destruction all these years, maybe I'm not seeing myself clearly here as well.*

I swallowed the pill. I crossed the line.

Some of my friends at the time were not supportive of me going as low as I did for as long as I did. They questioned my diagnosis, my approach, and asked me what the hell I was doing to myself. But they didn't have a clue what I was really doing to my wife and family. They did not know who I really was behind closed doors. It was not their family on the line; it was mine. If going low was the only way I would become a person my wife and family would choose to be around, then going low it was going to be.

BREAKFAST WITH DAD

My father knew I was going through a difficult time. He lived about an hour away. He called shortly after Kathy and I split up. "Can I drive up and meet you for breakfast?"

That began a weekly time with my dad when he would drive up early morning to have breakfast with me. In the beginning, it was pretty miserable, sad conversations over coffee. I did not know why this was happening "to me." The food tasted like sawdust in my mouth. Nothing like a hearty breakfast with a side of depression.

It was a comfort to me just to have him there. Many years had passed since those terrible days as a child. God had done remarkable things in my dad's life since that time. At this stage of his life, his heart had softened. He was repentant and seeking restoration between us. Those trips every week were tangible evidence that he actually loved and cared about me.

When I told him my bipolar diagnosis, he was not surprised. He shared his mental struggles dealing with bipolar through the years. It helped to hear about this. Then our conversations turned. I started asking him questions about his childhood. About his journey into manhood and fatherhood. He filled in the blanks I'd had about why he left during my adolescent years. Things had been tense between my mom and him. He had great rewards at work but struggled to do anything right at home. As a result, he sunk himself into his career and bailed on homelife. Bailed on me. He shared the guilt that kept him from engaging with me when he visited me in Portland when I was first married.

Revelation flooded in as I learned of his own father wounds as a man. His self-perception. His insecurity and fears. The decisions he made as a man, a father, and a husband. I discovered the honorable and redeeming qualities I had inherited from him. In the midst of this terrible sorrow, God was forging a new relationship with my dad I'd never had before.

I went from resentment to gratitude for God giving me my dad. It reminds me of the Scripture about the adulterous woman's interaction with Jesus. She wiped her tears off his feet with her hair. "I tell you, her sins—and they are many—have been forgiven, so she has shown me much love. But a person who is forgiven little shows only little love" (Luke 7:47b, NLT). My dad loved much. I never felt judgment from him during our breakfasts, only compassion and patience.

It was an amazing gift in the middle of my darkest days.

CHAPTER 9
HOME AGAIN
GOD IS IN THE REDEMPTION BUSINESS

BOUT TWO MONTHS AFTER I STARTED MEDICATION, I ATTENDED the Heart of a Warrior men's retreat. There, God spoke to me about viewing my current circumstances as loving discipline and evidence of my sonship.

Right after He spoke those healing and reframing words, the horn blew to go to lunch at the retreat. I got up and made my way down the mountain. Going up the sidewalk toward the lunch hall, I noticed a robin on the grass near me. When I looked up, there were over fifty robins on the grassy hill next to me. A big smile stretched across my face.

NOT OUR FIRST RODEO

Our current separation was not the first time Kathy had asked me to move out.

As I've shared, we separated within a year of arriving in Raleigh after being youth pastors. During that time, I had cried out to God, asking for reassurance my marriage was not over. At the end of an abandoned parking lot near my tech job, I sat on the floorboard in the back of my Toyota van with the sliding door open. Staring into the woods with tears streaming down my face, the sun lit up the Bible on my lap.

My eyes fell on Haggai, a book in the Old Testament. Chapter two, verse nine jumped off the page like it was illuminated. God Himself came into my Toyota van to answer me directly regarding my marriage.

"'The glory of this present house will be greater than the glory of the former house,' says the Lord Almighty. 'And in this place I will grant peace,' declares the Lord Almighty" (Hag 2:9, NIV).

I was reassured that separation would not end in divorce. We were reconciled two weeks later. This Scripture was a promise about my marriage I held onto through many tumultuous years.

Ten years after our first separation, here we were again. Only this time, my resolve to hold onto my marriage promise from Haggai 2:9 would not even last a year.

As a result of taking my medication, my thoughts stabilized. By the tenth month of being apart, reality finally set in. No Bible promise was going to pull my family out of the pit I had dug with my own hands.

For years, I held onto this secret promise from God that our home would be a place where His glory would be revealed. It would be a place of supernatural peace. I was a fool. It was time to let go of this false hope.

Even though Kathy had not legally filed separation papers after ten months, there was no sign of reconciliation. We did not talk. We exchanged kids when my visitation time came. It was clear, we would be divorced, it was just a matter of time.

During those months, my medication drastically changed my manic, volatile demeanor. I was chill for the first time in my life. I stopped driving toward anything. I had no ambitions at home, at work, in ministry, or in my life. I stopped fighting everything and everyone. I just was.

After a year had gone by, Kathy and I ended up on the back porch of our house chatting. I was returning the kids from a weekend at my place like any other time. After five months of being emotionally chill on medication, I guess she felt safe enough to invite me to stay a moment.

She looked amazing that night. Through everything, my physical attraction to my wife never stopped. If anything, it grew during our separation.

Our little visit was a tiny crack in the door of hope.

Our separation continued, now lasting over a year, into the fall. Our periodic conversations got longer. We kept the kids' visitation schedule, but I started to be around the house a bit more. The topic of reconciliation started to come up. She suggested instead of me signing another one-year lease on an apartment, maybe I sign a shorter-term lease. Another hopeful sign. I found another place with a shorter-term lease.

It would be another whole year before Kathy felt safe enough for me to move home. I continued taking my medication through this time.

As our separation got closer to the two-year mark, I found myself visiting home more and more, leaving for my apartment after the kids went to bed. It was not an abrupt change for them when I eventually returned home for good.

Just before the two-year mark, we met with a non-Christian marriage therapist to negotiate a moving back contract. The signed document was practical, non-spiritual, and clear. He continued to work with us for a few months after I moved home.

A NEW NORMAL

Moving back was a wonder. God in His mercy had been working behind the scenes in Rayn and Avi's life. Right before our separation, they were invited to be a part of an Assembly of God traveling kids' ministry called Kidz Ablaze. During the darkest times in our family, my two older kids (Rayn was thirteen; Avi twelve) got deeply involved and were loved by Pastor Randy. He saw the giftings and callings on both of my kids. The ministry would travel one or more weekends a month to do kids evangelist crusades. They did drama, skits, plays, prayer ministry, worship, dance, and many children came to the Lord through them.

When Kathy and I were in no state to pour into their lives, God was pouring into them, sustaining them through Kidz Ablaze and Pastor Randy. They were very aware of what was happening at home, but this ministry provided them a grounded God experience through it all.

When I moved back in, Olin was eight, and Abrie was six. Because of their ages, they were somewhat sheltered from the deep trauma that was occurring in our home during that time.

It was as if we were a normal family again. We spent the end of the summer and early fall on the boat, wakeboarding and tubing. Rayn was accepted into a magnet high school for modern dance. She continued to dance from the time we went to "The Call." Avi was on the starting line-up for the school football team as a linebacker. Olin continued to play ice hockey in local leagues and was the lead scorer as a center. Abrie was having fun all the time and along for the ride.

Kidz Ablaze started a Christian TV show that was syndicated around the US. Rayn and Avi played lead roles in the main cast. Rayn wrapped up every show with a Bible lesson; Avi was lead actor in multiple episodes and part of the main cast in support roles. They shot two full seasons of twenty-two episodes each.

We did everything together as a family. These were remarkable days.

Kathy and I had multiple honest and tearful conversations with the kids during that time. I confessed my abusive ways and asked their forgiveness. The kids noticed that I remained calm day to day. I put them to bed, prayed for them, mowed the grass, and did home repairs. Life was normal thanks to God's intervention and my medication.

Grateful just to be home, I put away all thoughts of ministry or God's calling. I enjoyed the everyday miracle of my family being back together.

God even restored my career. I was approached about another job. It was a senior management role at a competitive company overseeing technical marketing engineers. I was hired with a huge bump in our income.

During this season, I traveled internationally to many countries including Barcelona, Vancouver, Paris, Amsterdam, and London in addition to several trips to the San Francisco area where the company was headquartered. I always brought gifts back for the kids and when possible, Kathy joined me on these adventures.

God redeemed everything and great was the peace in our home.

RETURNING THE SIGN FROM GOD

Sometime after my wife and I reconciled, I heard that Walter's wife was dying. He was the guy who gave me the plaque two years earlier that read, "The greatest thing a father can do for his children is to love their mother."

The plaque was a treasured possession, a sign of hope for all God had in store for my family.

The plaque did not belong to me; it was a short-term entrustment.

My wife and I went over to Walter's house where his wife was in her final hours. We walked into their bedroom, and it was clear she did not have much longer on this earth.

I hugged Walter and told him I had something for him.

When I handed him the plaque, he started to weep. He said, "Thank you so much, you have no idea how special this is to us."

I thanked him for giving me something so valuable to their marriage when I did not deserve it. "You entrusted it to me for a season, but it is time for it to return to its original owner."

We all wept.

TRAINING FOR WAR

CHAPTER 10

LEAVE THE AMERICAN DREAM

GOD FAVORS THE BOLD

AN I BE HONEST FOR A MOMENT? MOST OF MY LIFE HAS BEEN A complete crap show. A multiyear series of train wrecks. Faceplant after faceplant in my marriage, my fathering, and my life.

I am under no illusions of grandeur anymore. God has shown me incredible mercy. Every day as I reflect on His kindness in my life, gratitude wells up in my heart.

"But God chose the foolish things of the world to shame the wise; God chose the weak things of the world to shame the strong" (1 Cor 1:27, NIV).

I am one of the fools who is dumb enough to believe God could do something amazing out of all my fatherhood faceplants. You may say, after all the hurt and pain I've caused in my family, isn't it best to just fade into the background? Sounds logical, but it is not God's call to a dad.

"But God." Don't you just love that part of the verse? But God specializes in strengthening the weak and using fools like us to express His great wisdom.

One of the beautiful ways God works is giving grace to the humble. There is nothing more humbling than face planting. In failure, you learn your limitations, your need for a savior. You learn that without God you are sunk. All the pride you had is gone when you are exposed for who you really are. From that position, you are open to God's grace in your life. You are open to be bold. What do you have to lose after you've lost everything?

You have seen this grace in action, but maybe you did not recognize it as one of the oxymoron-ish ways God's kingdom works. Let me explain.

The ugly boy who takes the risks gets the pretty girl. The guy who asks gets the raise. The unqualified and quirky gets the title. God grants Peter a leadership position after being one of the biggest failure out of all the disciples. By human standards, Peter "deserved" the lowest rank because of his mistakes. But God grants him more, awarding his boldness. He ends up being the only human being to ever walk on water besides Jesus. I imagine the other disciples saying, "But Jesus, we did everything right and colored in the lines, why does Peter get to walk on water?" I imagine Jesus saying, "He was the only one to ask, and then jumped out and did it." I can see the other disciples' response now, "Huh?" Another Jesus mic-drop moment.

God's kingdom works in a particular fashion. To go against it is to go against God working powerfully in your life. To find it is to step into the jet stream with the wind at your back. What is the key to experiencing this?

God rewards boldness! It is one of the ways the kingdom works.

He rewards the audacious, the radicals, and the zealots. The fools who dare to believe Him for great things achieve great things. "The people who know their God shall be strong, and carry out great exploits" (meaning bold and daring feats) (Dan 11:32, NKJV).

What does all this have to do with being a dad? You raise children to be like you. If you have a phobia of bridges, your children will have a phobia of bridges. If you are timid, tentative children you will have. If you never stepped out as an entrepreneur like you dreamed, you pass down those same fears of the unknown. You fear financial ruin at every turn, guess what your kids will be like with money?

Here is the reality. Bold dads raise bold children. Fearful dads raise fearful children.

Look at the parable Jesus taught about the master and his servants in Matthew 25. I will paraphrase.

A master is going on a trip and entrusts his three servants with all his property. No instruction. No list of rules to follow. Just trust. Each servant gets different amounts to manage.

Two of the servants take all they received and seek to give their master a return on his investment. Which both do generously. One of the servants, scared of losing what little he had, does nothing with what his master gave him.

Here is the kicker to the story. The master returns and gives the servants who doubled his money even more possessions plus a total blank check of "come and live in your master's happiness!"

The servant who operated out of fear, lack, timidity, and safety— what happened to him? The master says, "You wicked, lazy servant . . . Take the bag of gold from him and give it to the one who has ten bags" (Matt 25:26, 28, NIV). What the what?

I thought God was a kind grandpa who gave an equal amount of candy to all the kids. Nope!

Then Jesus says something that if truly understood, could start a revolution. "For whoever has will be given more, and they will have an abundance. Whoever does not have, even what they have will be taken from them" (Matt. 25:29, NIV).

God favors the bold. God favors the brave. God favors dads of action and not those deliberating about if it's God's will or not, all the while doing nothing!

That is how God's kingdom works. Those who worry over scraps in life won't have any scraps left to worry about.

The depressed get more depressed. The discouraged get more discouraged. Things go from bad to worse. Those who fear financial lack, struggle financially for the rest of their lives. They settle for scraps.

While talking to people like this, the life gets sucked right out of you while they look for you to agree with their viewpoint on life and plight.

He is the God of all comfort but not the way the American dream defines comfort. As a good Dad, He is not going to coddle you for the rest of your life. He will karate chop the bag of Doritos right out of your hands. He will jolt you off the coach with His intensity and invite you into a grand adventure with a loving smile.

Raising kingdom kids takes a dad who kicks passivity in the face and takes action. You've seen my faceplants. To lead from the front is a high-risk venture. I have a long list of failures. But God qualifies the unqualified, equips the unequipped, and calls us dads to lead our families into great exploits. That was exactly where God was taking me, putting everything on the line.

A DANGEROUS CONVERSATION

After I moved home, life was great. We found new rhythms of grace with each other. We were blessed in every sense of the word. God was restoring and rebuilding what was destroyed over the seventeen years of a volatile marriage and family life.

But God.

There were deeper levels of healing that still needed to occur. Kathy and I had abandoned our hearts' dreams. I had deeper fatherhood lessons to learn. Life with God never stagnates. The call is always to go farther up and further in. It's almost like He looks back with a twinkle in His eye and says, "I have something else I want to show you."

Three years after I moved back home, our oldest daughter Rayn was graduating high school. She did not know what to do. As Kathy and I prayed about it, we both got the same wild idea. What about the Youth with a Mission (YWAM) based in Kona, Hawaii? Kathy and I had always wanted to work with YWAM missionary organization since before we were married.

They ran a six-month discipleship training school (DTS) broken up into three months of Bible training and three months in a foreign nation doing evangelism and mercy ministries. It would be a great place to go as Rayn figured out her next steps.

Our twentieth anniversary was coming up around the same time, we decided to get a twofer. Take Rayn to Kona, say our good-byes to our first to leave, then tour around the Big Island and Maui.

Growing up, all Kathy ever wanted to do was go into full-time ministry, but because of my diagnosis, my emotional instability, and my spiritual weirdness, she basically said, "Forget that."

So there we were in Hawaii, enjoying the beauty, and God surprised my wife.

Right when we are dropping off my daughter at YWAM, God put a thought in my wife's mind. *You know, this could be you. Do you want to do this? I haven't forgotten your dream of going to YWAM.* That was it. That was all it took. It is just like the movie *Inception*.

The Holy Spirit drops a thought in your mind. It grows, expands, and consumes you until you face it head on and wrestle with God about it. She dealt with this for three months before she hinted at what was going on with her and God. It was so cute. She played the "I think God told me something but I want Him to tell you" card. I was like, *Crap, what if I lose in this game show called "What Did God Say?"* I had certainly lost that game before, so I was not keen to play it again.

Instead, I told her my Elkanah story from when we were separated. How God spoke to Hannah and Elkanah followed God's leading through his wife. I repented for being so spiritually arrogant, thinking God would use only me to direct our family.

That way of thinking is not being the biblical head of the home; it is just plain pride. God can speak through your kids, your wife, your parents . . . heck, even a donkey. (See Numbers 22 for that story.)

I asked for her forgiveness, which she gave. She proceeded to tell me she believed God was calling us to be missionaries. Seriously? You're kidding, right?

God was not clueing me in on any of this. The only thing on my mind was pushing for my next promotion at work and more money. My dream of ministry was left in the dust years ago along with the associated disappointments. I had no intention at this stage of my life of leaving the American Dream to pursue God in this way.

I started to pray about it. The most interesting thing happened. My desire to do it went through the roof. I never heard God speak as I had before, but my desire to do it was crazy strong.

Before Kathy ever married me, she'd wanted to serve as a missionary with YWAM. She imagined reaching unreached tribes with the gospel and living an adventure. That was over twenty years ago. Her life with me had killed that dream. But God! But God was bringing back Kathy's dream, letting her know He had not forgotten it.

The more our desire grew to become missionaries, the more fear took hold. *This is impossible. We have two kids in college, a mortgage, I'm almost fifty with a twenty-year career in technology.* I saw financial needs everywhere I turned. We didn't have money for this. Olin and Abrie were deeply engaged in school. Olin was entrenched in seven years of ice hockey, and he would have to quit. This was a major disruption to our life that I was not asking for.

Kathy asked the Lord that I would be a strong leader about going to YWAM versus leaning on her. Because it was "her crazy idea." That would be a sign God was giving us the green light.

From our initial conversation, Kathy and I wrestled with whether we should go now or wait another year. In a year, Rayn would finish YWAM and start college. Avi will have graduated high school, also attend YWAM Kona for a DTS, then return to attend the university.

Twelve months later, I wrote in my journal: "I fear I will never have peace until I dare greatly."

FORTUNE FAVORS THE BOLD

Audentes Fortuna iuvat is a Roman legion proverb. It is translated as "Fortune favors the strong, the brave, or the bold." As I said before, God rewards boldness.

In a powerful scene in *Braveheart*, young William's dad had just died. William dreamed he was lying next to his dead father. His father turned to him, looked him straight in the eye, and said, "Your heart now is free. Have the courage to live from it." Then he awoke.

Look around. How many guys do you see having the courage to live from their hearts?

I was on my front porch having a cigar with the Lord, a regular practice, thumbing through *Mansfield's Book for Manly Men* by Stephen Mansfield. I read maxim number one. "Manhood is action."

On the porch, I pondered, was I going to be a man of talk or man of action?

Then God walked into my thoughts like a six-foot-seven-inch fat man with broad shoulders. It was about to get real, real quick. The bar room of my mind cleared out. No one was left in the peanut gallery. Just me and God, mono a mono.

What He said was brief and to the point. "I have called you to go. I have called you to lead your family to go. The decision before you is, will you obey Me or not?"

That was it. No reassurance to all my concerns. No answers to my questions. Just a clear line between following Jesus or not.

Do I lead my family toward becoming missionaries, even with all the unknowns? Do I decide to put my faith into action?

There was no peaceful feeling to follow. No reassuring prophetic words to go on. No dreams that pointed to the answer. No signs in the sky.

With a cigar in hand, I told God I'd go. I would lead my family toward His call to leave the American dream and go into missions.

Right then, I heard a rustling within the tree in front of our front porch. I looked up from my rocking chair. A robin flew out. Unbeknownst to me, it had built a nest in the only tree in my front yard. I smiled.

As soon as I told my wife, I pulled the trigger.

She gave me a reality check straight away. "Okay, if you are going to lead our family in this and you believe it is God calling us, you have to be all in. You cannot waver like you have this year. Too much is on the line." *Crap.* This started with her but it would have to end with me leading the charge.

In her own way, Kathy was asking me to get back on point and lead our family. In military language, being "on point" means you are the man who assumes the first and most exposed position in a combat military formation, the lead soldier when advancing through hostile or unsecured territory.

Here is where the rubber meets the road when it comes to showing my children what leading boldly looks like. I was being called back up into my God-given role to lead my family.

I had been on point many times in our early marriage, but led us off the cliff. There was a long list of fatherhood faceplants that was my success record. So this time, I figured the best way to avoid more face-plants and eliminate harm to my family was to do nothing. I was not thinking clearly.

I was the "mope around; I've never done anything right; honey, what do you think" guy. Just because we were back together did not mean everything was aligned right. I acquiesced the leadership role in the family, forcing Kathy to assume the role, which she did not want. Many men have done the same to "keep the peace" all the while, not engaging as God calls us to.

Going into the mission field would take my family right into hostile environments to bring the gospel to unsecured territories. One of the things God was restoring as a part of this call to missions was getting me back on point. I did not want that role again. God was challenging me, big time.

I accepted the challenge with trepidation. What if I was wrong, screwing up my entire family? What if they ended up hating God and me because I led them into a disaster that was never God in the first place?

We lived our safe, suburban life now. Why would I seek to lead my family into danger that could result in long-term financial and relational ruin?

I had a library of worst-case-scenario books that I could go into my mind and check out any time. Every book ended the same way, some terrible catastrophe where my leadership was to blame.

With visions of disaster dancing in my head, I started the application process. I heard there was a family-focused discipleship training school (DTS) we could attend. So Kathy and I applied for the YWAM Family Discipleship Training Program, similar to the ones Avi and Rayn attended in Kona, Hawaii.

Within a few months, we got accepted.

Only Kathy and I knew we were pursuing this. We had not told our parents or our children. Our pastors did not know. It was just too radical of a conversation to have at parties with neighbors or church friends who wanted to have meaningful discussions about the health of their lawns.

Our next step was to pull the kids in for a heart-to-heart about what we believed God was telling us.

I had Olin and Abrie come into the living room. Rayn and Avi joined by FaceTime from their dorm rooms. Kathy and I were on the same page, but she let me take the lead in the conversation.

The atmosphere was abuzz as the kids did not know what to expect. Could it be terrible news like they had suffered eight years prior when we told them we were getting separated?

I got right to the point. "Kids, your mom and I believe God is calling us as a family to go into the mission field."

You could have heard a pin drop.

I said it again. "Your mom and I believe God is calling us as a family to go into the mission field. We don't want to just do this, we want to hear what you think; we want you to pray about it; we want to hear what your concerns and thoughts are."

Silence.

Rayn was the first to speak. "What about my college? Will I have to leave school?" Avi expressed the same concern. Olin said, "This is when college ice hockey scouts seriously start looking at players. Will I have to quit? What about my hockey career?"

Abrie asked where we would go. We told her we would move to Kona, Hawaii, with one of the possible mission outreaches in Tanzania, Africa. Immediately, she said, "Hawaii? I'm in, how soon can we leave?"

Then the bigger questions came: What about the house? Would we have to sell it? What about all our friends? Where would we put our stuff? What about our dog Scout and our cats Momma Kitty and Clover? How would we make money? How would we survive? Would we have enough food? Will it be dangerous?

I was getting the brunt of all their fears, and I had no answers for them. I did not know if we could keep the house. I did not know if Rayn and Avi could continue university. I did not know how we would financially survive. I did not know the details of how school would be handled for Olin and Abrie. I did not know how Olin's hockey and school prospects would be affected. I did not know anything except I believed God was calling us to do this.

The whole conversation just exacerbated my fears and insecurity of being on point. When the conversation was done, my wife turned to me and said, "Well, that went well," with a smile. She was hopeful and at peace that this was God's will. I was sinking fast, cinder blocks tied to my feet.

Knowing time was against us, I set a go-no-go decision date one month from our initial discussion.

Our older two had seen Kathy and me in ministry together. They knew it was in our heart of hearts to serve God in missions, but this was a big risk to them personally. But it was more of a shock to Olin and Abrie who had not grown up with us doing any kind of church work. Olin even said, "Why on earth would we do this? We hardly do anything at church as a family," which was true.

As Rayn thought about the personal risk this could cause her, she recalled an encounter she'd had with the Lord in Cuba while on outreach with YWAM. She was having a difficult time on the mission field. On one particularly hard day, she was complaining to the Lord about it. Then God said to Rayn, "You going to YWAM was not just about you. It is bigger than you. This has been a dream of your mother's from years ago." A few weeks after our initial conversation, she called and told us she believed God wanted us to go. She would trust the Lord to work out all the details.

After our initial conversation with the kids, the Lord impressed on me to invite Avi to come with us. Before he went to university, he had expressed a desire to go to a Discipleship Bible School with YWAM after he completed his DTS. That very school was running in Kona the same time we would be there. I asked him to pray about leaving university to come with us. After several weeks, he said he would join us.

Next was Olin. Leaving hockey was a huge sacrifice. He was four-teen at the time and was distinguishing himself on the ice as a center with a traveling ice hockey team. After a few weeks, he came to us and said he was willing to lay down his hockey aspirations to go with us. It broke my heart. As a dad, I went to God again. *Are You sure You are calling us? Because it feels like I'm leading my family off a cliff again.* I got no answer. Just silence.

Would I continue to follow Him by faith or bail at this point because I had no practical reassurances? By God's grace, I had crossed the line of obedience. No matter what came, I would lead our family forward toward God's call into the unknown.

SALVATIONS AND DENGUE

Now, what about the money? The whole YWAM adventure would cost us $40,000. I don't have that kind of money! Kathy and I did not want to raise support. We took it to God. He said to ask others to help us financially and pray for us on the mission. It was really humbling because, in some cases, we made more money than the people we were asking for support.

Our next question: What about the house? Kathy and I both sensed we were to keep the house. But how, God? How could I maintain the expenses of our house and come up with $40,000? No response.

Finally, we made it public we were going to the mission field for a six-month Family DTS/ Outreach, possibly to Africa. We asked for financial supporters to join us. It opened us up to criticism from every-one. *Why are you sacrificing the children's future to pursue your selfish fantasies and adventure? If you are so convinced it is God, why don't you sell everything you have and not ask us for anything? Who do you think you are asking people for money, don't you have a good job? Why don't you come up with an entrepreneurial business idea like a responsible adult and not ask people for money?*

Oh, this following God business sure is fun! Being on point to catch the brunt of everyone's opinion was a real joy.

When you are a dad seeking to follow God, you will find He is not so concerned with your reputation. Following God will expose you to misunderstanding and judgment by others. Such is the role of the man on point. We take the brunt of the accusations and continue to move our families forward.

God arranged for Kathy's niece and nephew to move in with us a year prior to us leaving for the mission field. When we announced we were leaving, they decided to continue to stay in our house. They would take care of all the utility bills, our cats, and pay a little more against the mortgage. Our dear friends would take our Siberian Husky, Scout.

The miracle was happening. I asked for a sabbatical at work, hoping for a financial safety net at the end of our six-month mission. They told me no. If I wanted to go, I would have to quit.

I took the decision to Kathy, and we prayed about it. We both had a deep sense of peace that God was guiding us, and that He was not surprised by this. To follow God, I would have to quit my job and lose our source of income. We both agreed.

The day came for me to resign. I awoke to God's reassurance from the book of Daniel:

"'Do not be afraid, you who are highly esteemed,' he said. 'Peace! Be strong now; be strong.' When he spoke to me, I was strengthened . . ." (Dan 10:19a, NIV). I wrote my resignation letter and hit send. Burn the ships, there is no turning back now.

Everyone we told was afraid for us. How will you be insured? What about the kids' education? How will you keep your house? How will you make money when you get back? On and on people asked me questions I did not know the answer to. I was walking by faith and leading my family not knowing all the answers to everyone's questions.

I was able to scrape up enough to cover half of our mortgage while we were away, knowing when we got back, there would be no money left.

We left for YWAM Kona in September, meeting each financial deadline just in time, every time. We had until the end of November to raise the full $40,000. God provided half of what we needed through our close friends for each deadline. I contributed the other half of what we needed overall. By the end of November, we were all paid for.

The experience of going to YWAM was a major cultural shock. Our family had not lived in such close proximity to each other in years. Just being physically closer brought out the best and worst in all of us. God used it.

It was a godsend that Avi joined us for our time in Kona. It was a sweet time with family. When it was time for us to go on outreach out of the country, Avi would return to our house. He would spend Christmas with Rayn while we were on mission.

The family DTS ended up canceling the mission trip to Tanzania. They instead gave each family a choice between Uganda; Baja, Mexico; or the Philippines. God led us to go to the Philippines. In early December, we joined six other families and flew to Cebu where we ministered for over a month. Then Kathy and I were asked to lead three other families to the lower island of Mindanao. There was known ISIS terrorist activity in the south where they had just blown up a church. We said yes and went to the city of Butuan for a month of outreach, which was located on the north side of the island.

During our time in the Philippines, Abrie lost a lot of weight, and she was small to begin with. She was traumatized by the culture, bugs, dirtiness of everything, and slept with Kathy and me the entire time. Kathy was sick with a stomach parasite or a nasty cold almost the entire two and a half months we were in the Philippines. Despite these challenges, Kathy and Abrie did all the ministries activities (evangelism, orphanages, hospitals, slums, Church services, etc.), we had multiple times a day.

During the entire mission, I had this nagging voice in my head that said, "You led your family into this?" I felt helpless about Abrie's culture shock or Kathy's illnesses. Olin seemed to roll with the culture. He even ate the infamous Filipino street food balut. Balut is a fertilized developing duck egg embryo that is boiled and eaten raw from the shell. He also attended his first cockfight as one of the white guests of honor.

While we were in Butuan, two of our team members contracted Dengue Fever from infected mosquitoes. Dengue attacks your blood vessels, causing your clot-forming cells (platelets) to leak. This causes internal bleeding and could lead to death. Symptoms includes whole body rash like the measles, pain behind the eyes, headaches, severe abdominal pain, vomiting, and muscle, bone, and joint pain. The locals call it the "bone breaking" disease because of the internal pain. I took the team members to the hospital daily to get blood work. If their platelets levels dropped too low, they would require an entire blood transfusion to save their lives. It was touch and go for about ten days. Fortunately, they recovered and did not require any major medical intervention.

When our family led a team to Butuan City, we had two to three ministries a day. Our families did preaching, teaching, feeding people, and evangelism in prisons, schools, and neighborhoods. We passed out Bibles and did children ministries in the slums. We shared testimonies, did evangelistic dramas, prayed for the sick in hospitals, fed street children at night, and more. Because of American's military involvement in the Philippines since World War II, English is widely used and understood throughout the islands. Not everyone can speak it but they can understand it.

Anyone on our team, young or old, could volunteer to do any of the ministries if they thought God was leading them to do it. We had so much going on, anybody was welcome to jump in and help. Two of those times, Olin, age fourteen, who had struggled at times even believing in all this God stuff, volunteered to preach at two youth events. I was like, *Okay, let's see how this goes.*

The first event had about seventy-five teenagers. He preached an incredible message and then gave a call for people to respond to Jesus. Thirty-five teens came forward to receive Christ. My jaw dropped.

Next time, he volunteered to teach in a remote town near Cabadbaran City at a youth meeting. A local church had rented out a basketball gym in the community for an evangelistic youth meeting. We arrived at a packed gym of over four hundred young people. Olin preached again, and another thirty teens came to salvation that day. They started calling him Pastor Olin. God showed me anything is possible.

The next event was a great example of God using the weak (i.e. me) and showing His strength. Our team had been going into this rough neighborhood in Butuan handing out Bibles and praying for people door to door. The neighborhood was formed from an unreached tribal people who had come down from the mountains to the town looking for work but had nowhere to stay. Eventually, town officials intervened and gave them a place to build a neighborhood. After several days in this community, we had a nighttime evangelistic crusade on their dirt basketball court. There were music and games. Kathy was going to give her testimony, and I was going to give the final message with an invitation for salvation.

Kathy got up and talked about how there was a time she was challenged in her beliefs because of injustices she'd suffered. She talked about surviving emotional abuse and how she walked away from God as a result. Then she shared how God pursued her and wooed her back with His love, despite the heartache she'd experienced.

The testimony was about me being an emotionally abusive Christian husband. It was about how I drove her away from God, but the Lord rescued her.

No one had any idea she was talking about me. She was sincere and loving. She was ministering hope to the crowd. She had no bad intentions in sharing her testimony.

But the Devil's voice filled my head. All I heard was, *You are an awful person. Look what you did to your wife and family. God had to rescue Kathy from you because you are so terrible. You hurt Rayn. You hurt Kathy. Now you are going to gloss over all that and stand up here acting like you're some righteous person. You are a sham. You are a fraud. It is wrong that you say anything to them about God in light of how rotten a Christian you are.*

Then they passed the microphone to me so I could preach the good news to three hundred people on the dirt basketball court. This is what it is like being on point. The Bible calls Satan the accuser of the brothers in Revelations 12:10. It is in Satan's job description to accuse. He was working overtime on me. I felt so weak because Kathy's testimony was true. I did all those things. Now what was I going to do?

I stood up, took the microphone, and preached from my heart for the next thirty minutes. The presence of God was strong. Standing in His authority, I did not back down from remaining in my position on point for my family. That night, over sixty people came to know Jesus. Young, old, fathers, sons, mothers, daughters, children, and elderly. The spirit of God moved powerfully in that unreached tribal community. It was amazing!

God had fulfilled a lifelong dream of Kathy's to be a part of reaching an unreached tribe with the gospel. For years she led our kids to pray that the gospel reaches unreached people groups. Now, here we were as a family doing just that.

There is a fledgling church in that community now continuing the work of discipling believers run by the Filipino YWAM staff.

Our family saw over one hundred and twenty salvations during our time on Mindanao island. In total, the three families that came with us saw over two hundred and fifty salvations during that month. God moved powerfully despite our weaknesses.

Being on mission with my family was really hard. The stress of the whole experience uncovered hurt still left in our family that was covered over by our suburban lifestyle but came to the surface during our time away. For example, failures of me as a dad not intervening in bullying between my boys years ago led to deep, deep hurt in Olin that I was completely unaware of. Insert another fatherhood faceplant. Failures of me as a husband as I put the "mission and ministry" cart in front of the "marriage and family" horse. The whole experience was a crucible.

We ministered in the Philippines for almost three months between December and February. We returned to the YWAM base in Kona, Hawaii for one week of debrief with the family teams that had gone to Uganda and Mexico.

When we returned from the Philippines, it was clear God was not leading our family into long-term missions. All doors were closed. No signs were pointing to continuing in missions or ministry at all. Plus, our experience had taken a toll on our family emotionally and physically.

Kathy wondered if I would be able to transition back to normal life and was concerned for us as a couple. With YWAM, I had put all my eggs in that basket, thinking this was the first step into long-term missions and ministry for us.

When no direction came from God through prayer, I was extremely disappointed and lost. Kathy was at peace, feeling we were to return home. At least we had a home to return to.

Abrie loved the spiritual community and family purpose we had with YWAM. She longed to stay in beautiful Hawaii, where she lived her "best life." Olin was over it. He wanted to get back home and back to his old life in high school as soon as possible.

Rayn and Avi survived without us. Rayn was able to stay in university, and Avi got a job.

I had no desire whatsoever to jump back into the corporate technology world I had left. I had spent the bulk of my career running software development and technical marketing teams. I could not conceive of returning to normal life after such an epic adventure. Even with all its hardships, mission work gave Kathy, Abrie, Olin, and me a common purpose and vision.

During our final week of debrief, we stayed at the YWAM Ship mission based on Ali'i Drive in Kona. It was a breathtaking location. From our lanai, we could see breaching humpback whales while overlooking the crystal clear blue waters of Kailua Bay.

One morning during breakfast outside overlooking the ocean, I got an email from a recruiter at IBM. They said they wanted to talk to me about a job. In the last six months, I'd had no interaction with anyone from my former work world. This was the first I had heard from anyone. My first interview was held from our lanai overlooking the bay.

After we flew home, within two weeks, I had a full-time job paying me the exact same salary I was making before.

I received my first paycheck days before we were about to run out of money. God is that good! I spent months worrying about money.

What a waste of time! It is nothing for God to provide what we need if we would only trust Him.

God led my family into missions for several reasons. God fulfilled a dream in my wife's heart to go to unreached people groups in her lifetime. God showed my children He can be trusted and followed radically. God led us into deeper healing as a married couple and as a family. God called us to go to share His love with hundreds of people in the Philippines.

God called me to get back on point for my family despite my weakness, past failures, and reluctance. I stayed on point because of God's strength. I am a living testimony that when I am weak, He is strong. When I am unable, He is able. Without Him, I am a complete crap show. With Him, I am the dad I need to be.

CHAPTER 11

PLAY THE LONG GAME

GOD WORKS IN A MAN'S LIFE IN SEASONS

GOD DEALS WITH MEN IN SEASONS. PERIODS OF TIME WHEN THERE IS an overarching theme to the work he is doing in a man's life. Think of it as a sports season. Not every season is go time. There are seasons of rest, recovery, healing, and slowing down. God is concerned not just about you at the moment, but all those under your care. Your wife. Your children.

It is important to understand what season you are in to discern the good God is up to in your life.

Think of a running back getting a knee injury. He eats, sleeps, and breathes football. He loves the game and the roar of the crowd. Now he stews on the sidelines with a knee brace, asking the coach to put him in.

He spent a week working hard at physical therapy. Doctor says it would be three months to fully recover. He keeps insisting, "Coach put me in," before his recovery time is up.

If the coach gives in, the athlete will hit the field at a disadvantage. All it takes is one linebacker to go after the knee. Hit it at just the right angle. The running back will go down in excruciating pain.

The team doctor will declare he has a shredded ligament, damaged cartilage, and a dislocated kneecap. Then he will utter the word no athlete wants to hear, "You're done."

"With the season?"

"No," says the doctor. "With football."

That is how many men live. We play hurt. We feel better (i.e. no immediate pain) so we rush back out onto the field. We don't do the hard work of long-term recovery. We play the short game looking to accomplish what we can immediately, not thinking of the future ramifications.

God will not put us in the game hurt. You can ask, but He will say no if it is a season of healing or recovery.

Playing the long game means you take the time to fully heal, allowing God to form you into a man who He can entrust more to. Your focus seasons of downtime are about you having a long-term sports career. Or in this case, a long-term chance at being the dad your kids need.

I recall reading in a dad book once when my kids were young something to the effect that it is typically not the best time for you to try to conquer the world while your kids are very young.

I hated reading those words. When Kathy and I would go through good periods, I ran to achieve my dreams of ministry or other lofty aspirations because in that exact moment, things were good. I continued even though I felt the resistance of God and my wife that I was being too excessive and not focused enough on family activity. It never made sense to me. Why can't I just run after the things I want in life, whenever I want to? But dads need to work with God to learn how to focus their energy and effort and care for their family with all their heart. I was very binary. I was all ministry and no family. Or all family and nothing else. God wanted me to have the character to excel in family and in life.

It may mean sacrificing short-term personal adventure for long-term gains at home. God is a good Father and knows what we as dads need. Our coach knows there are no shortcuts in life when it comes to our character. That is what we will pass down to our children, the decisions and sacrifices we made to stay in the season God had for us.

Men, I would be lying if I said God's seasons are short. They typically are not. Real change in our hearts does not happen over a weekend or a month. Just like the seasons of the year, God works to transform our true character over periods of time.

Trust Him even if it lasts three months or three years. It will be worth it.

11:11

Failing as a youth pastor ended a season of trying to go into ministry in my thirties. I fell into a software quality engineering job thanks to my long-term friend Grady from UNC-Wilmington. My technology career helped meet our financial needs, but it never scratched the itch of having a purpose in life like ministry did. At the time, I did not see family as God's best work. I saw "platform ministry" as the only way to serve God. I wanted to be the preacher, the pastor, the evangelist with the microphone in front of thousands of listeners. I did not want to serve in some obscure or unseen way, I wanted the "God" spotlight on me.

When God called me to minister in Ethiopia, it was a dream come true. I thought finally God was going to allow me to walk into my dreams of missions and leave my technology job. As you know, that is not what happened. God in His mercy began to speak to me in an unusual way the summer before I left for Africa. He was preparing me for the season I was about to walk into.

John Mark McMillian's dad, a pastor at Morning Star in Charlotte, NC, shared in a sermon I was listening to about an experience he had after he left the ministry. When God was calling him back, he kept seeing the number 11:11 everywhere. He studied every 11:11 Scripture in the Bible. He concluded the "11:11 sign" meant restoration and double fruitfulness. It was an intriguing story; I did not think much of it at the time.

Suddenly, I got a call from my wife. She asked me to swing by the house and pick up two checks she had written to support some missionaries she knew.

As I went to deposit the two checks in the ATM, I noticed one check was written for eleven dollars, then looked at the second check. It was also written for eleven dollars. Man, you should have seen my face.

It was like a zoom in meme with Chris Pratt.

Then it began.

I would go to make coffee in the morning. I'd reach for a cup of coffee and the coffee-maker clock would say 11:11 a.m., yet it was 6 a.m. At some point, the power went out and reset the clock, but really?

It got ridiculous. "Your total is $11.11" as the cashier rang up my grocery bill. I'm driving down the highway, glance up, and the license plate in front of me has 1111. Glancing at the clock before I climb into bed, 11:11 p.m. This went on for years after Ethiopia.

One time, I quit a dead-end tech job because God had provided another tech job. I glanced at my phone right before I walked out the door: 11:11 a.m. My wife and I had a meaningful conversation about going to YWAM when we were still trying to decide. When the conversation was over, the clock read 11:11 a.m.

John Mark McMillian's dad said God was calling him back into the ministry when he started seeing these signs. I got my hopes up. Maybe that was what God was doing with us? As you know, my life went downhill fast after Ethiopia. I destroyed Kathy's children's ministry. My mission organization folded. Then Kathy and I split up three years later. It did not make sense.

After years and years of mystery around this, I finally got clarity on what God was saying, or more accurately, doing.

As the day approached for my family and I to become missionaries with YWAM, I started to reflect on when this 11:11 thing started in my life.

Then it hit me.

My family and I would arrive in YWAM Kona on September 27, 2018. I looked back at my old journals, and I saw I had arrived in Ethiopia on a call from God on September 26, 2007. I did the math, and it was eleven years to the day.

Wow! Only God could have coordinated that. I finally understood.

I would go through two significant seasons in my life. Eleven years of restoration followed by eleven years of abundance.

I never understood this sign was actual years of my life, years of restoration.

In those eleven years, I failed in every aspect of my life between the ages of thirty-nine and fifty. Family, marriage, career, ministry, friendships, personally, etc. So many years of fatherhood faceplants.

Any inch of pride and selfish ambition left in me was stripped away. I tried to do ministry in these eleven years after Ethiopia many, many times, but all my efforts fell flat and lacked God's touch. God turned my heart toward home in those years, teaching me deep truths about fatherhood that I am sharing with you.

You have to trust God's timing with you. He is interested in you having a long-term impact in your family. That may mean years of obscurity or years when your personal dreams are not being fulfilled. Trust God. He will give you something even more amazing than your personal dreams—His dreams for you and your family.

The level of gratitude in my heart going into missions with my family was incredible. It was so much richer and more fulfilling to follow Jesus together, sharing the experience with my kids. The eleven years of hardship were worth it. Embrace the season God has you in right now. He intends to richly bless you and your family if you submit to His fathering guidance.

CHAPTER 12

BE A LOVER AND A FIGHTER

YOUR PERSONAL VICTORIES BECOME
YOUR FAMILY'S VICTORIES

FOLLOWING GOD AS A DAD IS NOT EASY. PARENTING IS NOT FOR THE faint of heart. One of the recurring training modules God put me through is spiritual warfare. As a dad, you must learn how to wage war against your enemy. He will attack you personally and attack your family. God does not want your family left defenseless. One the fundamentals of getting back up after a faceplant is learning how to fight against the "spiritual forces of evil" as Ephesians 6:12 says.

Here are a few stories from my time in the fatherhood "cage fighting" octagon.

SPIRITUAL WARFARE, DAD-STYLE

During our time in Pittsburgh as youth pastors, Rayn had some demonic encounters at night as a four-year-old. Kathy and I were not well. I was desperately seeking other employment to get us back home to North Carolina. During that time, something was tormenting Rayn every night. After she fell asleep, something would come out of the wall, speak to her, and terrify her. Even in my faceplant state at the time, I had enough sense to pray in the blood of Jesus and command the demon to leave.

This went on for a week or two, then the evil thing left, never to return. She slept peacefully without fear from then on.

Years later, after we arrived back in Raleigh, Rayn had another encounter with the demonic. It was on the heels of some inner-healing I was seeking out through a ministry called Restoring the Foundations. This was before Olin and Abrie came on the scene. Kathy was away one night at work, and I put my older two down for bed.

That night, Rayn kept coming out of her bedroom, frightened and in tears, saying she felt like there was "something" in her room. I was so angry at the enemy trying to attack my children again. Plus I was hyper-aware of the enemy's activities because of the inner-healing ministry I was seeking help through.

Not on my watch—I had had enough!

I got her out of bed. Avi was already awake, so I got him out of his room too. I leaned down and told them about the power of speaking God's word out loud. I told them we were going to fight this together, even if they were in their PJs.

Rayn, Avi, and I marched around our first-floor apartment yelling and chanting, "'God has not given us a spirit of fear, but of power and of love and of a sound mind!' 2 Tim-o-thy 1:7."

We marched, doing call-and-response like in the military. I would yell and they would shout it back to me. This went on for twenty or thirty minutes. We got louder, more aggressive, and more joyful. The more we declared, "God had *not* given us a spirit of fear" the more the heaviness, the fear, and the spiritual tension in our apartment lifted.

We were not playing. This was not a game. This was not Scripture memory playtime with Dad. It was spiritual warfare!

My kids and I fought the demonic presence in our apartment until it was completely gone. My kids had big fat grins on their faces when it was all said and done. I asked them if they noticed a difference in the feeling of our home. They did. They both went to bed peacefully having defeated their first demon. Sleep tight, kids.

HOUSE ON THE HILL

Anyone that has battled sin, addictions, or a traumatic past knows life can get visceral real quick. It can feel like you're in hand-to-hand combat with the enemy of your soul and your family every day.

One night, I had a vivid dream where God pulled back the spiritual curtain to show me what was going on in the unseen around my home. This occurred sometime during the multi-year season when God was teaching me about the high call of being a dad.

In the dream, I owned a beautiful white one-story historic house like the ones you might see in downtown Charleston, SC or Savannah, GA. The white paint was peeling off in multiple places. The house had an inviting front porch with a swing. It was close to the sidewalk and had a little white-picket fence separating the house from the sidewalk.

From inside, I could hear demons yelling at me from the sidewalk in front of the house. They taunted me, threatened me, and called me names. Next, I heard windows breaking. They were picking up rocks and throwing them through the front windows.

I was too afraid to go to the front door and see them. In the dream, I knew they could not step onto my property, as though it was sacred ground on which they could not tread. The rock throwing and yelling went on for hours. They were destroying my home, piece by piece.

The next scene in my dream was of a beautiful grassy knoll. It was huge and rose high into the air, like something out of the Dr. Suess book *The Lorax*. At the bottom of the hill was a grassy field as far as you could see. The same white-picket fence from my first scene surrounded the edges of the property.

Way up high atop the hill sat the same beautiful white house. No broken windows. No peeling white paint. It was a bright and fresh spring morning. Birds were singing. I was suddenly inside. The smell of coffee brewing wafted through the air. Sunlight streamed through the windows. I walked onto the front porch.

Way down at the bottom of the hill, outside of the same white-picket fence, were demons pacing back and forth. They were yelling something, but I could not hear them. They were picking up what seemed like little pebbles and throwing them onto my lush green grass. They looked like little black dots. It was so far away, they were easy to ignore. I strolled back to the house listening to the birds singing. Then I woke up.

"The way of the righteous is like the first gleam of dawn, which shines ever brighter until the full light of day" (Prov 4:18, NLT).

God showed me in the dream where He was taking me. The house on the hill. A secure home of peace where evil does not torment, rage, or reign.

At the time I had the dream, I was bare-knuckle boxing with rage, anger, mental instability, and daily anxiety. Kathy and I were on the verge of our first separation, but I did not know that at the time. By the grace of God, the house in my dreams is where we live today.

It took years to move from the house with broken windows to the one on the hill. God trained me through experience how to fight and overcome spiritual forces of darkness that seek to "kill, steal, and destroy" me and my family (John 10:10).

As a dad, you need to wake up to the fact that the battle with your demons or the evil that has lurked in your family line is real. You will have to fight to gain ground; there is no way around it.

Be encouraged. You have the upper hand. You have the advantage. You have God Himself, the heavyweight champion of all creation, coaching you round by round in your corner. He already overcame the world as Jesus said in John 16:33. Now He is going to supernaturally strengthen you to do the exact same.

You will win over these troubles that plague you, taunt you, and throw rocks through your windows. You will be set high on a hill where no devil can touch you.

You are not an alcoholic just one minute away from your next drink for the rest of your life. You are not a sex addict just one step away from ruining all the victory you've gained over sex these last four months. You are not a Christian forever in hand-to-hand combat against your demons for the rest of your life. Your life verse is *not*, "I want to do what is good, but I don't. I don't want to do what is wrong, but I do it anyway" (Rom 7:19, NLT).

You are a Jesus-follower whose light is growing as bright as the noonday sun. That is the normal path of progress for the righteous. Your "mouths were filled with laughter" (Ps 126:2, NIV). In your house, you will hear "shouts of victory" because you are "more than conquerors" (Ps. 118:15, Rom 8:37, NIV).

Quick Bible lesson: when you accepted Jesus, you became righteous. "For our sake he made him to be sin who knew no sin, so that in him we might become the righteousness of God" (2 Cor 5:21, ESV). Your life changed from being one step away from a drink that will destroy you to living way up on a hill in a beautiful home. You are thousands of steps away from the sin that wants to destroy you. The demons still exist but not on your property. Not where God has raised you up. Jesus moved you out of the hood to a house on a hill far away from what used to torment you.

Our life as Jesus-followers is not always on the edge, one inch away from disaster around every turn. Living in the tight quarters of sin management, afraid to move too much lest we fall off the cliff, taking our family with us. God is taking you to a place that has room. A home where there is freedom to roam and run. Yes, a place where even mistakes can happen without the hammer coming down. Life and death does not hang on every decision or lack of decision you make. "He brought me out into a spacious place; he rescued me because he delighted in me" (Ps 18:19, NIV).

God is so good to us. He takes the janky thing called your life and turns it into the most beautiful, poetic, and powerful testimony the world has ever seen. When you start to get victory, round by round, your focus turns from your personal fight to the ones you are fighting for—your wife and your children.

You become a lover and a fighter.

GOD DROPS THE MIC

"The true soldier fights not because he hates what is in front of him, but because he loves what is behind him." —G.K. Chesterton

That is the shift every dad and husband must make. It is not just about you anymore.

You overcoming your demons is not about your personal happiness, peacefulness, and stability. The house on the hill in my dream was what God wanted for my wife and children. A home full of life, peace, stability, safety, laughter, and fun.

You start to awaken to the fact; your victory becomes their victory. Ground you gain becomes the ground your children gain.

As David, the warrior king, put it, "I pursued my enemies and overtook them . . . I crushed them so that they could not rise . . . I beat them as fine as windblown dust" (Ps 18:37, 38, 42, NIV).

Do you think God gave you masculine intensity and divine strength to do nothing with? God wants all your heart to join Him in going after every devil that plagues you and your family. Run toward the battle. Kick open the picket fence at the edge of your property and chase the demons down. Beat them until they are no more.

You will not overcome the enemies of your life and family in your own strength. You must run toward the battle in the strength God gives. King David is a perfect example of this.

David was the youngest son in his family. His older brothers fought in the king's army. Saul was the first monarchy over Israel, detailed in the book of 1 Samuel. David's father sent him to bring his brothers supplies and get word of how their current war with the Philistines was going.

When David arrived, he saw a giant warrior named Goliath taunting King Saul's army to come and fight him one-on-one. He came out every morning and evening, threatening Israel. Each soldier was afraid, including David's older brothers. But David's righteous anger was aroused when he saw the situation. I felt this way when Satan tried to attack Rayn in our apartment.

David said, "Who is this uncircumcised Philistine that he should defy the armies of the living God?" (1 Sam 17:26, NIV).

Even though David was young and scrawny, he ran toward the fight. He did not go full steam ahead relying on himself. While he ran, he declared, "This day the Lᴏʀᴅ will deliver you into my hands, and I'll strike you down and cut off your head" (1 Sam 17:46a, NIV).

What an example of emotional intensity, physical weakness, and audacious faith combined in one verse. We have access to the same power when we face the evil that confronts us.

Why? Because we are provoked by love. David was provoked by his love for God. Evil better never dare to come after my kids, my wife, or onto my property again. That is the emotional intensity love brings to your fight. You have a reason bigger than your own personal freedom to win the battle.

All of my Christian walk, I viewed my struggle with sin and temptation as a very private thing. Just me trying to work it out with God. Until God showed me an obscure verse in the Bible that rocked me. I glanced over it until God nudged me to go back and read it again.

"For God will save Zion and rebuild the cities of Judah. Then people will settle there and possess it; the children of his servants will inherit it, and those who love his name will dwell there" (Ps 69:35–36, NIV).

Doesn't that just jump off the page and grab you?

Honestly, the bomb did not go off for me until the Spirit of God showed me the treasure buried in this easy to overlook verse.

Here's how it went down.

GOD: Who are the people?
ME: Mothers and fathers of godly homes (i.e. Zion, Israel)
GOD: What does it mean to possess it?
ME: They fought off the enemies that were on the land and claimed all the territory You promised to give them.
GOD: Who inherited what they possessed?
ME: Their kids
GOD: The children of the righteous will inherit the land their fathers possess.

God dropped the mic. I sat there in stunned silence as spiritual grenades went off in my heart.

I gained understanding that the land represented the life I could have in God. The house on the hill. Overcoming sins, living in a spacious place and walking in victory. The amazing kind of life Jesus talked about. "I have come to give you everything in abundance, more than you expect—life in its fullness until you overflow!" (John 10:10, TPT).

God will not drop the amazing kind of life into your lap. Instead, God looks you right in the eyes with His hands on both sides of your face and says, "You got this." You then turn around and see a guy twice your size ready to rumble. Imagine he is the sin you are struggling with. Faith is believing you got this because God said you did and you start swinging.

All of this is a gift from God. Your strength, your faith, your ability to engage all come from the Lord. As John the Baptist said, "A person cannot receive even one thing unless it is given him from heaven" (John 3:27, ESV). Victory is gained through faith in action. In other words, putting God's gifts to work in your life.

When you get the victory, there's another guy three times your size. God reminds you that you've got this and you go at him full speed. You do that enough times, before you know it, you will have the abundant life Jesus said He came to give you.

There's one critical piece to this, though. As a dad, you have to engage. No house on the hill awaits the man crouched down, covering his ears. While the home is filled with the sounds of breaking glass, you rock back and forth praying, *God, make it go away*. The empowerment God has given you as a dad is to engage. Take steps of faith against the spiritual forces trying to oppose you.

As you saw in my story, the opposition in my life was not Kathy. It was the evil that sought to overwhelm me and, subsequently, my family. Guys, it is not your wives who do not agree or see things your way. The battle is not with them. The battle to obtain the house on the hill, the family you always dreamed about, is within you. Your goal is to say the same thing Jesus said about himself.

- "The prince of this world is coming. He has no hold over me." John 14:30 (NIV)

- "The ruler of this world approaches. He has no power over me."
  John 14:30 (NLT)

- "The ruler of the world is coming, and he has nothing in Me."
  John 14:30 (NASB 1995)

When you start to live in all the promises of God. That is when you turn to your kids and tell them, "You got this." You overcame giants and now you are raising future giant-killers. As a dad, you hand down the personal victories you gain in your life as their inheritance. It becomes their starting place, their starting block.

You cannot guarantee they will not sin or screw up, but you've removed the generational obstacles. Now they can run their race of life without hindrance inherited from you.

Jesus gave us a key to overcoming sin. "Therefore, since Christ suffered in his body, arm yourselves also with the same attitude, because whoever suffers in the body is done with sin" (1 Pet 4:1, NIV).

If you are willing to starve your sinful desires to gain a better life, you will overcome the demons that plague you.

Let me assure you, after winning a few battles, the victory becomes easier. As the Bible encourages, "His commands are not burdensome, for everyone born of God overcomes the world" (1 John 5:3–4, NIV).

God says winning and following Him are not burdensome. Believe it by faith. It has been my experience the battle intensity changes as you gain more and more *W*s.

It will feel like stepping out on your porch, in your house on the hill, in the morning; cup of coffee in hand, sun rising, and seeing the demons off in the distance at the bottom of the hill. The words they speak you can barely hear and are easy to ignore. The temptation they offer seems so small, so far off instead of big, in your face, and overwhelming. There is a spacious place between you and them in Christ. It will take more effort to go and engage in sin than not to. The battle does not stop, but the intensity of the combat will.

I'm not perfect, but I have gained some ground back in my life. So will you, but you have to be willing to do the hard work when it's time to engage.

One last thing. Hopefully you have noticed that God likes to ask questions. He reveals the truth through inquiries. Many times, we look for blunt-force conversations with God. *Stop! Take the job! Go here! Do that!* None of our other relationships are like that, but we tend to want God to interact with us that way. As you've seen in my life, God wants to converse with you. God wants to honor you in this way. Be open and ready for God to drop the mic in your life when you start to listen . . . really listen.

CHAPTER 13
FACE YOUR BATTLES
THREE BATTLES EVERY MAN MUST WIN

F YOU FOLLOW THE WELL-WORN PATHS OF YOUR FOREFATHERS, YOU will find yourself in the same ditches they did. The good news is, you can be different. You can build a better life. Our lives were ransomed once and for all from "the empty way of life handed down to you from your ancestors" (1 Pet 1:18b, NIV).

Part of our salvation is to save us from living an empty way of life that will never satisfy and always ends in frustration. Sex is the answer. *No it is not.* Money is the answer. *No it is not.* Fame is the answer. *No it is not.* My wife agreeing with me is the answer. *No it is not.*

Being older, I have a perspective I did not have as a younger man. That is a nice way to say, I've had more time to screw things up and learn how God can fix and redeem everything.

My heart for you is this: you don't have to learn the hard way, unless you have to learn the hard way. You know who you are. Pain is sometimes the best teacher.

While writing, God brought me to a Scripture in the Bible more than a few times. Ezekiel chapter thirty-three.

It is a story about a guy selected to go up on the wall and look for enemies coming to attack the city. He is called a watchman on the wall.

The watchman is not ignorant or inexperienced. He has seen and lived some life, so he has a keen eye for how the enemy will attack. In this book, I'm that guy.

As the dad, you are the man on point. You are the gate to the city called your family. You are the target for most spiritual attacks. But many of us are clueless there is even a war raging around us, let alone at us.

Sometimes, when I meet a younger man, I can see myself in him. I think, *He is going into life with no idea how brutal it's going to get.*

Honestly, I think ignorance is a gift from God. Not ignorance of the spiritual battle but lack of awareness of how much they will have to fight to truly overcome. Looking back, if I'd known the hard work ahead, I may have opted out of the journey.

As younger men, God invites us into the adventure of . . . marriage, providing, parenting, purity, and power in our private lives. It looks so inviting and exhilarating. Then God starts the training modules, to make us the warriors. Do it again. Do it again. Do it again until we get it right.

The taste of sweet victory in Jesus comes after the bitter taste of your own inability, weakness, and faceplants.

I'm going to make it plain. There are three battles you will have to face and overcome to live in the house on the hill with your family.

The battle for identity, the battle for validation, and the battle for allegiance—Jesus faced these battles. The good news is your Coach knows how to win these battles. He is your trainer for the match. Once you overcome, you will get to teach your children how to, as well.

THE BATTLE FOR IDENTITY

Your first and most significant battle is the battle for identity. If this is out of whack, what you pass down to your children will be as well.

Your identity is not your natural talents and skills. Your identity is not your spiritual anointing or gifting. Your identity is not the titles you hold or the results you produce. Your identity is not your God-given calling or assignment. Your identity is not your marital status.

Your identity was settled before you did anything in this world. I will say it again. *Your identity was established before you did anything.*

God said to Jeremiah, "Before you were even born, I knew you" (v 1:5, NIV). That is for all of us, not just special Bible people. How could God know us before we even knew ourselves? Mind-blow.

What God knows about us is actually the great discovery of our lives. Have you ever talked with your kids about memories you have of them when they were little, before they even were conscious of what was going on? They have no memory of birth, ages one or two or three.

It is a fascinating topic to your kids because you hold special keys that unlock their identity. You sat outside of their conscious experience of themselves. How much more can God! Before you were even born, God knew you.

God the Father told Jesus the Son and everyone listening, "This is my Son, whom I love; with him I am well pleased" (Matt 3:17, NIV). Jesus had done nothing at this point. No amazing ministry or work to warrant such love. He had not overcome Satan's temptations. He had not sacrificed Himself. He had not helped others through miracles. He had done nothing. Yet God was pleased and loved Him because He was His Son, that was it.

God feels the same about you. He loves you because you are His son.

One thing that is true: identity is elusive.

It seems you can grasp God's perspective on who you are one minute and lose it the next. To stand firm in who God made you to be will take a fight.

Satan's bull's-eye is on your identity. It is one of the key ways dads can faceplant. Seeking identity in the wrong places will have unforeseen consequences on your kids. Years after being in technology, before we got separated, I would see sales people doing very well for themselves. I fancied myself a high-flying, jet-setting, traveling technology sales person. To be flush with cash and go exotic places would be good for my ego. Plus, it would get me out of a tense marriage situation at home, so I thought. God in His mercy never allowed it. Had I pushed the issue,

I would have repeated the same faceplants my father made during my adolescent years.

I was seeking identity in my accomplishments at work—very common amongst dads.

This is a battle you must win so your kids can have victory in overcoming lies that will come to attack their identity. God wants to use you as a dad to help establish this God-given identity in your kids, but it starts with winning your own battle for identity.

This is key because having a God-given identity causes you to be unshakeable by circumstances. Having an identity based on the "empty way of life handed down from your ancestors" is completely dependent on your life situation. Who are you when you are broke, unemployed, underemployed, obscure, have no platform, are not heard or seen by others? God-given identities don't change even when life does.

As my family and I considered being missionaries, we had a few fits and starts along the way. A year before we became missionaries, we had attempted to go to YWAM Kona. We got accepted into the Fire and Fragrance DTS. The F&F discipleship training school was 99 percent unmarried young adults in their teens and twenties. They were in the midst of a massive revival, with every evangelistic outreach they were involved with blowing up with thousands of salvations in different locations around the world. The leaders were all in their mid-twenties. We as a family would be an awkward fit because of our age and life experience. After we got off the phone with them, my wife thought it was not the right time to go. She also did not feel F&F DTS was the right environment for us.

Avi was graduating high school and his next steps were unclear. My wife wanted to ensure we were around as he took his next steps after high school. I had no sense from God what to do. So I made the call to stop the application process after my wife's wise and discerning counsel.

But I had so much false identity wrapped up in this decision. When I canceled our plans, I was crushed. This was my chance to leave an empty work career behind me and do what I've always dreamed of, go into the ministry. The timing of this event coincided with a year-end review of my work performance in my new role as a product marketing manager. My director told me I could not write worth a crap, which was critical to my job's success, and it appeared to him my heart was not in the work. Both were true. I got an average rating for the year's work, no bonus, no incentives, and no hopes for future advancement. To my identity, I just got my report card, and I failed.

Seemed like God was not interested in me serving Him after years of doors shutting in my face and work was merely putting up with me. Satan smelled blood in the water and went in for the kill.

Note, the Devil has one or two core moves when it comes to attacks on your identity. For me, Satan's core move against my identity was rejection.

Here is how it played out. I was driving down the road, after I had quit my dream of becoming a missionary, with thoughts of my failing report card at work. I was distraught. It seemed the things I wanted most in my life never happened. I was feeling hopeless. I was at my end.

A scene of a boxing ring formed in my head while I was driving. It was so vivid. To use charismatic speech, I think I was having an open vision. In non-spiritual language, man, my imagination was going wild while I drove down the highway.

The scene opened with me getting smashed across the jaw by an enormous fist. Sweat jumped off my face as my body slowly twisted toward the floor. I landed with a tremendous thud and my body bounced slighted off the mat.

I did not want to get up. I could hear my trainer from the corner of the ring yelling in slow motion, "Get Up!" I lost count of the number of rounds I had gone at this point. My face was flat on the mat. My mouth guard hung out of my mouth, drool.

I heard my thoughts. *I can't do it anymore. I can't. I'll just lay here and the blows will stop. Every time they land right where it hurts. Every time!*

As I laid there, time stood still. The pain of the blows sunk even deeper. The scene seemed so visceral, real, and targeted. With my face flat on the mat, I recounted the bout play-by-play. Every jab delivered with an identity crushing message of rejection.

A knee to the chest—"Everyone has rejected you." A right hook across my jaw—"Your family has rejected you." An uppercut to the chin—"Your friends have rejected you." Several quick body blows—"No one wants to hear anything you have to say." A jab to the forehead—"Your work doesn't want you." And a final hit below the belt—"Even God does not want you."

It all felt so true. It seemed I had spent the better part of my life in this ring getting pummeled. The vision was like a metaphor for my life. Then the fight against my identity would subside as if I was not in a ring at all.

I'd have time for bruises to heal. I'd have time to regain my strength and stamina back. Then unexpected circumstances would occur, hopes and dreams dashed, identity shaken, and out comes my opponent. *One-Two, One-Two-Three* nailing the same spots over and over.

So here I was again. I wanted it to be over. I thought of options to end this life-long battle. "I'll just stop trying. I won't care. I'll stop training. I'll stop fighting, then I won't have to face my opponent. I'll stop pursuing God's call. I'll stay below the radar. I'll get by. I'll settle."

Like a smelling salt, I heard the voice of my trainer again in slow motion, *"Get Up!"*

The referee started the count *one, two, three . . .*

Still facedown, I thought to myself, *I may not have the strength to fight this battle.* The count continued, *four, five.* But I found the strength to get up. *Six-seven.* I decided to not give in. Not today. *Eight-nine.* Not ever. With the little strength I had left, I stood.

Boxing gloves by my side. Sweat dripping off my body. A bloody cut above my left eyebrow, dripping into my eye, made it hard to see. I stood in defiance.

As I lifted my face, I whispered, "It's not true."

My opponent cocked his head with a grimace. "What did you say?"

Again, "It's not true." Then louder, "It's not true!" Then even louder, "It's not true!"

My opponent flies at me. With gloves by my side out of exhaustion, all I could do was proclaim the truth.

I *am* deeply loved! I *am not* rejected! I *am* accepted! I *am* chosen! In my periphery, I see my trainer jumping around, his arms in the air, rejoicing with songs of victory! (Zeph 3:17, NIV).

My opponent swung with all his might, but he could not get near me. His gloves did not touch me.

I won.

From my youth, Satan has hit me over and over again in the same old bruised spots. But no more. Today I got up in the midst of the fight. I did not stay down for the count. I heard the voice of my trainer, my Father God, from the corner of the ring saying, "Get up!" And I did.

Your identity is Satan's primary target because all else flows from that central place.

Do you know who you are? Can you defend your identity against all the attacks that will come your way? If Satan can capture your identity, then all the other dominos in your life will fall. Your allegiance to God will crumble because if God does not like you, love you, or is mad at you, then why bother? Your thirst for accolades and respect drive you to poisoned wells to drink. Then you will drink and join the walking dead.

I won the victory in the car. I fought against the lie that God rejected me and did not want me, the same way I had felt all the other people in my life had rejected me at one time or another.

Satan wanted me to align my belief to a lie based on my current disappointment.

Satan is opportunistic and jumps on circumstances to continue this campaign against you. Face every disappointment with the truth of God's word about you, stand strong, and you will overcome. In His perfect timing, a year later we ended up going to YWAM Kona.

Your identity must be based on God's love for you as His son or you will lose this critical battle every time.

Jesus fought Satan's accusations against His identity during His temptation. "If you are the Son of God . . ." the gospel of Matthew chapter 4 reads. The Devil was pointing at His circumstances of hunger to question what His Father said about Him. Jesus fought Him with Scripture He believed. He will teach you to do the same.

Are you a sinner who occasionally gets it right or a saint who occasionally gets it wrong? This is a key question many have written about and discussed. The Devil wants to tie your circumstances to your identity. If you sin, you are a sinner. If you do righteous things, you are a saint. Who would ever win that battle? No one!

That is a losing strategy. If you want to win the battle of identity and subsequently lead your kids to win the same, you have to start from what God says about you. You are a saint who occasionally gets it wrong.

I am not saying you are sinless, but your core, God-given identity is a saint, a righteous man. Your fight is to become who God says you are, to act like it, smell like it, and talk like it.

Don't believe me, believe the following Scriptures that define who you are:

- In Jesus, your identity is "blameless" —Jude 1:24

- In Jesus, you are the "righteousness of God" —2 Cor 5:21

- In Jesus, you are "righteous and holy" —Eph 4:24

Now put on your boxing gloves, get up, and fight to align your life to your God-given identity. In turn, you will be able to train your children how to win when the enemy comes after their identities.

As I shared before, God showed me one way to fight for my children was to draw them each a word picture of how God saw them. Through the years, I reminded them every chance I could what God said about them. Not looking at their current behavior or circumstances, instead I reinforced their God-given identity, no matter how it looked on the outside. Years later, Avi, who was not a perfect kid by any stretch, remarked how he always knew who he was. Even when his behavior did not align to his identity, he knew he was not acting like his God-given self.

THE BATTLE FOR VALIDATION

The next battle you will face is the battle for validation.

Many times we seek validation through accolades. The quest for the roar of the crowds, the approval of men, and the respect of your peers. I know we are no longer in middle school, but it sure does seem like it sometimes.

I run a podcast and online community called the Kindling Fire. It has been a journey of humility, testing my motives, and learning to be at peace. I thought I was starting the show and community for others, but in fact, I was about to be schooled again by God through the process.

It started out well. I had many friends with amazing God testimonies that the world needed to hear. I started a podcast to interview them so they could brag on all God had done for them. I did not have huge expectations for the results, but then again, I did.

Everywhere I turned, there was another story of "I sneezed and gained one million followers on Instagram." Or "I just threw this video up, and it went viral." Success in social media was so effortless for so many. I had hoped it would be true for me.

Nope. It did not happen.

I quickly got into the pit of the "not enough" syndrome. Not enough likes, listeners, subscribers, downloads, readers, and views. I obsessively checked my podcast and subscriber statistics. Every day was another indictment of no one being interested in what I had to offer.

I attended entrepreneurial e-courses, read blogs, and my misery got worse. Underneath my pure motives for starting the show was the thirst for accolades, for validation. I am worth something because I was "successful."

I tried every technique they suggested to grow my subscriber list. Design your funnel. Use social media influencers. Try harder, do more, keep at it, ugh! Someone please get me off this desperate success train I bought a ticket for.

In an honest moment with the Lord, I told Him I was miserable. I was perpetually disappointed.

The more "famous" people I got on my show, the more depressed I got. My high expectations dashed each time.

God, in His love, said, *Why did you start all this in the first place?* "Because I had friends with amazing God stories that others needed to hear." He told me, *Instead of reaching for the "stars" in this world, be faithful with what I've called you to.* So I was.

Then I started to experience this deep sense of fulfillment and joy in the show. I stopped looking at my statistics all together. I set myself free from the "Am I important?" social media scorecard and just enjoyed what God had given me.

The more I let go, the more God brought people to me and blessed the show. The more I strived for accolades, the more miserable and disappointed I became. With God's help, I had won this battle.

You are faced with the same battle every day.

Will you advance yourself, promote yourself, or let God move you forward in His way, trusting in His timing and the level of success He wants for you?

Jesus faced this battle when He was tempted in the desert. Satan suggested Jesus go to the highest point on the temple in Jerusalem and jump off for everyone to see. Prove the Scripture about angels catching you and then *BAM!* your ministry will take off.

People will follow You, talk about You, and think You are the chosen one, just like that. The temptation was to take His ministry, His dreams, His calling into His own hands and accomplish it Himself.

That is clearly the world's way for Jesus, but it is not His Father's way. God's way took longer, was confusing, and more painful. Yet when Jesus resurrected from the dead, I could imagine God saying to the world, "I bet you didn't see that one coming."

God has a plan for you and your children. We must trust His process to lead us to fulfill it. You know you have won the battle for validation when you stop trying to arrange for life yourself. You allow God to lead instead of driving yourself toward some false image of success or validation.

FACE YOUR BATTLES

Your children will face the same temptations to seek validation in what others think of them and in their accomplishments. When you win this battle, you can in turn show them what the world holds up is a false promise. You can lead them to be true to their God-given talents and ability. You can show them being true to God's plan for their lives is the most satisfying way to live. The best teacher is your example. Show them your belief in how you live out your life, the decision you choose to make knowing God has validated you already.

Your children are growing up with social media measuring sticks in their face every day. Help them be free from the prison that seeks to define their value from what others think of them or what they accomplish.

When you personally win the battle for validation, you don't pass on this empty way of life to your kids.

THE BATTLE FOR ALLEGIANCE

The last battle you will face is the battle for allegiance. Will you lay down what you want for what God has for you? I would describe this level of commitment as the fear of the Lord.

"The fear of the LORD is the beginning of wisdom" (Prov 9:10a, NIV).

Like the dirty Santa gift exchange, it can feel like you are losing out when God takes the gift in your hand and gives you another. You shake it, you lift it, and it does not seem as good as the gift He just took away. That job, that house, that church, that relationship, that blissful igno-rance, . . . You want your old life back.

You pray for God to return your old gift. You pray He will allow you to peek into the mystery gift He has handed you so you can see if you want to keep it.

You look over at crazy Uncle Bernie who just opened up his gift. He got keys to a brand-new car. What! You know Uncle B is a terrible driver. How did he get such a generous gift from God? How is he so blessed and here you are with this crappy thing, I don't even know what it is.

You shake your box again. Probably got some useless gift like hand-kerchiefs or something.

131

Oh, how the Devil loves these moments. You actually don't know what is around the corner with God, what gift He has in store for you and your family. You gave Him your Christmas list in prayer, but will He answer like you want Him to?

You have desires, but does God care about those? He just took the gift you thought you wanted or needed right out of your hands. That job you wanted. That promotion you wanted. That success you longed for. That perfect marriage. You have nothing in hand but this mystery gift. That is when the Devil whispers that God does not care for you or for what you want.

The Devil accuses God. His arguments feel like the truth, but they are a lie.

Jesus dealt with feelings of doubt. Right before He was going to the cross in the Garden of Gethsemane, He struggled. Is this the only way, Father? Is there another way?

"He fell with his face to the ground and prayed, 'My Father, if it is possible, may this cup be taken from me'" (Matt 26:39a, NIV).

He asked His Father three times, but God said no each time. There was no other way to fulfill His mission but through the cross. This was the ultimate battle for allegiance.

In the end, Jesus declared, "My Father, if it is not possible for this cup to be taken away unless I drink it, may your will be done" (Matt 26:42, NIV). He won the battle. His allegiance would be with God and not to save His own life.

As a dad, you may not face life-and-death decisions like Jesus, but you will face the crossroads of where your allegiance lies. Your children will come to that cross in their own life as well.

Personally, becoming a long-term missionary was a dream of mine for decades. Yet God sent me back to the corporate "salt mines." Have you ever been disappointed by God like that? He takes away the very thing you long for and says He has something better for you.

The gift you wanted, He exchanged for another one He picked out just for you.

That is when allegiance gets put to the test. You will face that moment in your life. You will fight that fight.

God's goodness will be on trial in your mind when circumstances don't go your way. Just like when I was separated. Learning God's judgment and discipline of my behavior was His mercy. He was saving not only me but my family as well. It is incredibly painful. Like the cross, it killed every sinful, fleshy part of me. Yet without that death, there would be no resurrection.

If you don't overcome being God's fair-weather friend, you will pass on a half-hearted faith to your children. When God disappoints you, you'll bail. Victory is not secured across generations by fathers who quit when the going gets tough.

What you pass on to your kids is what is in your heart. There is no way around it. What is inherent to who you are. They can choose to not follow your half-hearted ways, but it is what you pass on if you don't win this battle.

Even if there are fatherhood faceplants here. God is a God of redemption. My whole life is one big example of mercy and restoration that I never deserved. Get back up and face the battle for allegiance again until you overcome.

In Psalm 16:11, David said of God, "You have shown me the path of life."

God wants to lead you down the path to an abundant life. It will not make sense to you in the beginning or even while you are going through it. Show your allegiance by staying the course.

Trust Him, God is taking you somewhere good. Satan offered Jesus a shortcut by tempting to give Him the world if only He bowed down to him. Jesus won that battle and He will lead you to win your battle for the allegiance of your heart.

Expect the test. It is coming if it has not already come. I believe you will pass it through faith expressed in allegiance.

When you do, turn to your children and help them navigate their allegiance when God's ways do not make sense to them. When they want to chuck the fear of the Lord out the window. Your testimonies will encourage them. God works miracles when we persevere. I know, had I bailed out sooner, I would not be walking in the blessings I have now. The same is true for you.

Give the gift of an authentic faith to your children. One that sustains them through hard times. Winning the battle for allegiance gives them confidence. If God was faithful to you, He will be to them.

A VICTORIOUS LEGACY

CHAPTER 14
REPAIR THE BREACH
STAND YOUR GROUND, AFTER EVERYTHING, STAND!

FIRST THINGS FIRST. HEALTHY, HOLY, HEALED, AND HAPPY DADS raise mighty kids. You may not be any of those things right now. Thankfully, Father God initiates, trains, and guides us to become those dads. His training starts with teaching us to engage, to fight, and to gain small victories. After that, He leads us where the fight is most intense, the breach.

As a single man in my twenties, I went up for prayer at the end of church service for my struggle with porn. Every guy I knew struggled. The man I asked to pray for me was in his late sixties. I briefly explained my request to him. He looked at me with sad eyes and asked if I would pray for him for the same issue after he was done praying for me.

Are you friggin' kidding me? It's hopeless! You mean I am going to struggle with this until I'm dead. *Shoot me now, this gospel must not actually work,* I thought. Talk about disheartening. Sadly, my tale is not uncommon. As a younger man, I longed for someone to be an example, not to just talk but to show me how to walk out this good news.

Since that time, I've met so many men who are free from the sin of porn and many other secret sins, as I have been by the grace of God. They are shining examples of a God that is stronger than sin. Yes, it's true there is power in the gospel to overcome rage, anger, porn, abuse, pride, covetousness, and so much more. If God did it for me, for the men I know, God can do it for you.

As a dad, how do you overcome in life and not be overcome? How do you walk out a life stronger than the most heinous sin that is common among us? Then, in turn, pass on those victories to your children?

The first step is dealing with the breach in the wall.

BE A WATERSHED MAN

I recently went hiking with an old college friend and he told me this story. After his recent divorce, he finally had confronted his dad about porn. His father was into hardcore triple XXX plus porn and had been for most of this life. He found out this was one of the spiritual inheritances he received from his father.

It was no surprise then to hear my friend had a long history of struggle with this sin before, during, and after his marriage ended. The same demons that ran my friend down were the same ones that ran his father down throughout his life.

He then went on to tell me, he stayed at a friend's house when he was in his twenties. He was activated in the room he was staying in and knew there was porn hidden somewhere. Sure enough, between the mattresses was the friend's dad's stash.

How did my friend "know" it was there? There was a spiritual breach in the wall in that home. An access point for this sin.

Whether you like it or not, you will pass down your secret sins to your children. Anger, lust, pride, lying, all of it will be given like an awful gift to your children for them to have to overcome or be overcome by. You will raise your kids with the same breaches in their walls, unless you close them. That is the power God has given you as a dad. For good or evil, you will have an impact.

This spiritual truth is why you see families characterized by the same sins generation after generation. Womanizers, unfaithfulness, porn, alcoholism, physical abuse, depression, and the list goes on. The breach in the wall remains open generation after generation. The demons go in and out like a revolving door.

What is a breach in the wall?

I was reading the Bible one morning not expecting much. In military fashion, the Holy Spirit snuck up on me and set off a truth bomb regarding the breach from Isaiah 58.

"You will be called the repairer of the breach, the restorer of the streets in which to dwell" (Isa 58:12, NASB).

Dads are like a wall around a city. The role of a wall is to protect those who live within it. Those on the wall, the watchmen, are always aware of threats or danger on the horizon. A wall is strong and tall. It is built to withstand battle and confrontation. God builds us brick by brick, stone by stone to become this barrier for our families.

Those within the walls experience peace and joy. They live in complete freedom. No need to consistently look behind them or check over their shoulder. A strong wall provides a positive environment within the walls.

What is the atmosphere like in your home? That is a good indicator of the health of your wall.

A breach is a broken portion of the wall that gives the enemy access to those who live within it.

The breach is secret sin. God knows about it. Satan knows about it. You know about it. It could be obvious stuff like Galatians 5:19 lists out: sexual immorality, sexual impurity, lustful pleasures, sorcery, hostility, quarreling, jealousy, outburst of anger, selfish ambition, envy, drunkenness, and so on.

It could be subtle sins like acquiescing the role God has given you as a father in the home. Passivity in stepping into your place at home.

Either way, the breach is the issue. That is where our Father will take us to fight.

The breach may have been caused by your father's or grandfather's sin, like a shoe through drywall. It could have been caused by your own decisions, sin, or lack of action. Either way, the effect is the same. It is an access point to your family.

If it is a multi-generational breach, the fiercer the battle. You are confronted with generations of fathers who never closed it. Your role is to close it for the generations that follow you.

As long as a breach remains, there will be consequences in the home. Evil operates on authority. As a father, you have spiritual authority for good or for evil. You are the wall around your family.

"For where you have envy and selfish ambition, there you find disorder and every evil practice" (James 3:16, NIV). Notice how unseen sins (envy) show up in behavior (evil practice) that can be seen. That is the way it works.

It is just like gravity, nothing personal. It is the way God has made the unseen world to operate. If Satan was successful in overcoming your ancestors in a particular sin, it is highly likely he will come after you in confidence expecting your surrender just like all your forefathers did.

Never surrender! Never give up!

This is where you take your stand, with God at your side. This is where watershed men are made. This is the weight room of fathers who say no more! The pattern of compromise and sins stops here, in this generation. No longer will I allow this breach to remain in my family's life. It stops with me.

Dads who wage this war are watershed men.

When your fight is bigger than your personal sin or holiness, you are fighting for destructive generational patterns to break once and for all. My children will not start with a breach in their wall in this area of their lives.

You have your eyes set on the prize promised. God shows "love to a thousand generations of those who love me and keep my commandments" (Ex 20:6, NIV).

You are fighting for redemption of your last name. When people utter your surname in the future, it will be characterized by strength, vitality, righteousness, joy, peace, laughter, honor, nobility, and a warrior-like spirit. No longer will your surname be associated with womanizers, alcoholics, secret porn addicts, short-cutters, liars, connivers, hot-tempered abusers, emotionally unstable, arrogant people.

This is the hill God has been training you to take. He has every weapon and tool you need. Repairing a breach will require you to fight and rebuild at the same time.

In the book of Nehemiah, it said he carried the burden that the walls were broken down around Jerusalem for months. It weighed heavy on him. You will feel the same burden when you start to wake up to the fact that the breaches in your walls are negatively affecting your family.

Nehemiah could not close the breaches in the wall around Jerusalem by himself. He asked for help. Men rallied around him to rebuild the wall. It is an awesome picture of men fighting on behalf of one another. You need other men to cover your back and fight on your behalf while you, with God's help, repair the breach. They also need you to fight on their behalf.

> Therefore I stationed some of the people behind the lowest points of the wall at the exposed places, posting them by families, with their swords, spears and bows. After I looked things over, I stood up and said to the nobles, the officials and the rest of the people, "Don't be afraid of them. Remember the Lord, who is great and awesome, and fights for your families, your sons and your daughters, your wives and your homes." When our enemies heard that we were aware of their plot and that God had frustrated it, we all returned to the wall, each to our own work. From that day on, half of my men did the work, while the other half were equipped with spears, shields, bows and armor. The officers posted themselves behind all the people of Judah.
>
> —*Nehemiah 4:13–16, NIV*

Don't you love that God frustrated the enemy's plot to keep the access points open? He will do the same for you. He wants your walls rebuilt, and they will be.

It took God eleven years to rebuild them in my life as I had breaches all over the place. I learned to walk openly with other men as I worked to repair breaches in my life. As one repair finished, He would go to another area of my life that needed attention. He will do the same for you. I had a spear in my hand while I built with the other hand. That is the posture of a watershed man. I had men championing me on my rebuilding journey. Throwing spears through the chest of my adversaries when they came to attack. I also fought on behalf of my brothers. I had their back, they had mine.

Repairing the breach is done in a community of warriors. All being trained by our Father.

With God's help, I overcame a violent temper, a cruel tongue, emotional abusive patterns, a porn weakness, passivity, giving my leadership role and responsibilities to my wife, unwise money practices, excessive anxiety, fear of man, arrogance, fear of intimacy, fear of weakness, lying, and so many other areas.

It takes time for God to rebuild a destroyed city.

God will direct you how He wants to help you close the breach in your walls. As the example found in Nehemiah, it is best done in a community of warriors.

Here are four ways God helps you to close the breach in your walls. I learned this from John Eldredge's book *Waking the Dead.*[2] It is called the four streams.

1. Walking with God: Learn to hear and obey God's voice in a particular area.

   - "My sheep know my voice." —John 10:27

2. Counseling: Hear God's voice through trusted people.

   - "Hear counsel, receive instruction, and accept correction, that you may be wise in the time to come."
   —Proverbs 19:20

2. John Eldredge, *Waking the Dead* (Nashville: Thomas Nelson Publishing, 2006). Used by permission. Text included is paraphrased.

3. Inner Healing: Understand where your heart is wounded. Uncover lies you have believed about yourself, others, and God. Exchange your brokenness for God's wholeness and truth.

   - "He has sent me to bind up the brokenhearted."
     —Isaiah 61:1

4. Spiritual Warfare: Learn how to fight and overcome the enemy's tactics against you.

   - "For our struggle is not against flesh and blood, but against the rulers, against the authorities, against the powers of this dark world and against the spiritual forces of evil in the heavenly realms." —Ephesians 6:12

I encourage you to get *Waking the Dead* to dig deeper into how these four streams look and work.

DON'T EXPECT A COOKIE

When you decide to be a watershed man that closes off every access point that has run in your family for generations, brace yourself. Evil will test your wall's strength. Demons will mock your resolve. Stand strong and you will overcome for your sake and the sake of your kids.

God told Jeremiah, I will make "a bronze wall" and your enemies will "not overcome you."

"Get yourself ready! Stand up and say to them whatever I command you. Do not be terrified by them, or I will terrify you before them. Today I have made you a fortified city, an iron pillar and a bronze wall to stand against the whole land—against the kings of Judah, its officials, its priests and the people of the land. They will fight against you but will not overcome you, for I am with you and will rescue you," declares the LORD.
—Jeremiah 1:17–19, NIV

When you decide to guide your family in a new godly direction, don't expect applause, expect opposition, accusations, and resistance. Don't expect a cookie. Remain loving in all you do and after years, people will start to recognize you did something different. They will start to notice how your children are distinguished among their peers or in life. That is the fruit of hard work done by a father who closed the breach in his walls.

I will say one last thing. Closing the breach in your wall does not guarantee your children will not sin or love God with all their heart. Each person is free to choose God or not.

By doing the hard work, you are giving your children the best starting block position in life they can have. You removed obstacles in their race. You are positioning them for the win. With no extra baggage from you and no huge barriers in front of them, they can run their race as fast as God designed them to.

God fathered me when I needed it the most, so I became the dad my children needed. He was loving them by loving me. He is ready to do that for you.

CHAPTER 15
LIVE UNCOVERED
DADS MUST OVERCOME GUILT TO ENGAGE

CLOSING THE BREACH PROTECTS YOU AND YOUR FAMILY FROM frontal attacks from the world, the flesh, and the Devil. But the enemy has more subtle tactics.

There is nothing that will undermine a father more than dad guilt from faceplants. I believe it is the number one reason for male absenteeism and passivity in the family. The ever-present awareness, *I screwed up*. The longer it goes on, the deeper the gulf gets between a man and his children.

Take my dad's awkward hug as an example. When he visited me in Portland, I needed his full presence and strength. The pressure was enormous, and I felt so unprepared. I barely knew how to keep my bills paid, let alone raise a healthy family.

I knew why he was guilt-patting me—all the anger, all the physical abuse, and all the other crap. But I didn't need all that. I needed an engaged loving dad more than a guilty, unresolved, half-hearted father. A man who had made it right with God so he could be strong and make it right with me.

Your kids need the exact same thing.

But how?

Grab your cigar and come by the campfire. It's time for a lesson from the good ol' Bible. What I'm about to share will make the difference between you stepping into your full masculine self as a dad or you shrinking back into less.

"Every man who prays or prophesies with his head covered dishonors his head" (1 Cor 11:4, NIV).

Right before this verse it clearly says, "the head of every man is Christ." So, to pray or prophesy with your head covered dishonors God. That is pretty clear, right?

What does praying with your head covered even mean? This verse has perplexed me for twenty years. I never heard a sermon about it. I have no idea what it means but it seems to be an important key for men to unlock something in their lives.

OVERCOME DAD GUILT

I was reading about David's life and a small detail about his physical appearance jumped out at me. He was the most famous king in the Bible and wrote the majority of the book of Psalms.

I read, "David continued up the Mount of Olives, weeping as he went; his head was covered . . . All the people with him covered their heads too and were weeping as they went up." (2 Sam 15:30).

So here is the sad scene, it will take a bit for me to set the stage. All these stories are from 2 Samuel.

King David, as a young man, loved God. God loved David and gave him a kingdom after many years of testing. God said, "and if all this had been too little, I would have given you even more" (2 Sam 12:8, NIV). King David was a passionate warrior who ran with a crew called the mighty men (2 Sam 23:8).

King David's heart started to wander after God gave him multiple wives, money, fame, extravagance, power, influence, and so on. Instead of engaging in combat as he had done alongside his brothers, his mighty men, he decided to sit back and enjoy the luxurious life he had.

While his valiant men engaged in battle against Israel's enemies, King David hung out by the pool.

While on his pool balcony, he saw and lusted after a woman he had not slept with. He already had many wives, and she was married. Her name was Bathsheba. He seduced her and got her pregnant.

Adding insult to injury, her husband was fighting on David's behalf, sacrificing his life to honor the king. David had fallen far away from the man of integrity that God entrusted so much to. To cover up his sin, David ordered the husband be killed, which he was.

Through a prophet, God confronted David. David repented, married Bathsheba, then the baby they conceived died.

Many years later, David's sin revisits his family. One of his sons, Ammon, rapes one of his daughters, Tamar. David was furious but the Bible says he never did anything about it. Tamar's brother Absalom wanted David, his dad, to exact justice on Ammon, his half-brother. But he never did.

Why did David not intervene to discipline his son Ammon?

He felt guilty, that is why. He did nothing because who was he to stand up and tell Ammon he had sinned? When he had done even worse by killing a man after he slept with his wife.

Absalom was devastated at David's inaction. So he planned how he would get revenge on his half-brother. Eventually he kills him in cold blood, two years after raping his sister.

David's guilt and subsequent inaction made his family situation worse. When he followed God, he was a man of action and integrity. Now he was passive, reluctant, and guilt-ridden.

After he learned of his son's murder, he moans but never engages. Absalom flees the city after the crime. David never reaches out to Absalom, yet weeps of his lost relationship in the privacy of his palace.

As a result, Absalom's hatred for his dad's passivity and lack of engagement grows. Eventually, David's military general steps in to help out the estranged father-son relationship by convincing Absalom to return to the city. For three years after his return, David refused to see his son.

Why is David acting this way? Guilt. A large self-awareness of his own unworthiness. He was convinced he caused all this havoc in his household in the first place.

Absalom, fueled by a father wound, turns the heart of the city away from his dad. He gets an army and overthrows his dad's kingdom.

Returning to the sad scene I started with, David and his entire household flee the city. The king was afraid his son Absalom would come into the palace and slaughtered everyone by the sword, including David, had he stayed.

Along the road he walked, feeling sorry for himself. He was weeping and covering his head because of the shame of his fatherhood faceplants.

We are like David. Covering our heads because of our sins, yes even as Jesus-followers. Not engaging. Not doing the hard work of fathering when we are needed the most.

With heads covered, we decline the invitation from God to engage. We sit in our self-pity and say they would be better off with someone else as their dad. No mountains are moved on behalf of your household. No prayers are uttered except, "God have mercy on me, a poor sinner."

God invites us to join Him in declaring words of life over our family. Prophesying them unashamed. We stick next to David with our heads covered and wonder how we could ever stand up and do that. Look at the mess we've made. We cannot.

We are dishonoring God. No good for ourselves. No good for others.

Dad guilt is a sin. We need to repent of it. It robs us from leading our family. It honors God to receive forgiveness and uncover our head. We must step into our God-given strength as a father.

None of us are without faceplants, but only those who uncover their heads and engage become the dads our children need.

Praying and prophesying with our head covered means approaching God and others from a shame and guilt perspective.

This undercuts more men than probably anything else. We men are passive as we replay our sexual failings, our angry outbursts, our broken promises to our kids, and our long list of other sins.

We think we must have lived a righteous life for us to be powerful. So we limp along playing an old worn out record in our head, "Oh have mercy on me." At least we are not causing more harm by disengaging in life, but, in fact, we are. Our lack of action in the lives of those God has entrusted to us adds insult to injury.

Brace yourself, men, because it is about to be real. I'm not talking to the ignorant, unaware of their sin. I am talking to you who are very aware of your sin and your failings.

"How much more severely do you think a man deserves to be punished who has trampled the Son of God under foot, who has treated as an unholy thing the blood of the covenant that sanctified him, and who has insulted the Spirit of grace?" (Heb 10:29, NIV).

Oh, you haven't trampled on anything, you are just feeling sorry for yourself at your family's expense. Stop it!

Every day you don't receive full forgiveness and redemption is another day you hurt others through passivity. You will go about your religious activities covering your head, idling in neutral, and going nowhere.

What is at stake? Your life and the life of generations that follow in your footsteps.

Guilt and regret rob you of standing in your rightful place as a husband, father, and friend. Jesus has freed you. Mercy triumphs over judgment, condemnation, and accusations.

Take off your head covering. Engage with your family in confidence. God the Father is poised to give you strength and courage today, if you repent of treating the blood of Jesus as an unholy thing.

Satan hates you and has an awful plan for your life. He desires you beleaguered, tired, beaten down, disengaged, and depressed. He has a highlight reel of your fatherhood faceplants on repeat. It is his specialty to keep dads down in the doghouse of life.

All the while, our kids and our wives call out to us, "We need you!" We stay in the doghouse by choice, hurting everyone and ourselves.

Aren't you sick of it? I'm done with living like that. Jesus broke death's back so our sins would never hold us down.

The world may say, "How dare you? Who do we think you are?"

We reply, "We are the soldiers of our Lord Jesus Christ. We are an unstoppable army. We take ground and don't give it back. We advance. Evil retreats. We are new creations who are not bound to allegiance to our old passive, sin-loving nature. Our hearts are good. Our hearts are new. Our hearts are pure. We love God and love others. We are beloved sons and warriors. We are valiant. We are noble. We are kings. We are the Devil's worst nightmare. We are fathers. That is who we know we are."

Men, Jesus' blood bought your masculine and spiritual vitality back. It's time for you to take hold of it and live uncovered.

CHAPTER 16

RUN FREE

GOD PROVIDES THE DESIRES OF OUR HEART

NOW THAT WE ARE ALL AMPED UP, LET'S TALK ABOUT HOW TO fully engage within God's guidelines. I'll start here. "The boundary lines have fallen for me in pleasant places" (Ps 16:6, NIV).

I have to be honest, for years I hated that Scripture. If you are in that boat, then you can join the party. But don't get too excited because the potato chips are stale, the Coke is flat, and everyone is grumbling.

When I read that Scripture, I did not hear provision, care, and ease. I heard restrictions, limits, and rules. How can I be free yet live within some type of constraint? It does not make sense. Yet according to Scripture, boundaries can be good. I did not fully buy into this truth until recently.

A year ago, my wife was out of town and my kids were gone for the weekend. Freedom! I could do whatever I wanted, whenever I wanted. There would be no commentary, no restrictions, and no boundaries.

So I did.

I woke up the next morning with one thought. *I'm such a loser.*

The house was a complete disaster. I did not clean a dish or find the trash can all weekend. I stank from chain-smoking cigarettes. I was exhausted from binge watching *Stranger Things* until I-don't-remember o'clock.

I was trying to lose weight at that time. I had a friggin' bread fest that weekend and my gut was jam packed. Beside my bed was a family-size bag of Doritos that did not have a chance.

My next thought, while I laid in bed, was this Scripture, "The boundary lines have fallen for me in pleasant places." There God is again, coming into my mess with His love.

I would never have behaved that way had my family been home. Abrie with her innocent eyes, *Daddy, why are you killing yourself with cancer?* Kathy asking, *Are you really going to eat again?*

As I laid in my bed of regret, God and I had a conversation.

GOD: Are you better or worse with your family around?
ME: Better.
GOD: Family is a boundary line I placed in your life for your good.

Finally, I understood God's boundaries in my life made me a better man. Left to my own devices, diabetes here I come, with a side of lung cancer please. God in His wisdom sets boundaries for you so you will grow as a man and as a dad.

We are free to do whatever we want that is within biblical morality but Scripture warns us to be wise with our freedom. "'I have the right to do anything,' you say—but not everything is beneficial. 'I have the right to do anything'—but not everything is constructive" (1 Cor 10:23, NIV).

A boundary-less life is not God's best for you or your family.

You may hate the restrictions and limits God puts around you like I did, until you start to see the why behind the boundaries. God is providing something to you and your family, not trying to keep something good away from you.

No, you cannot take that exciting travel job. No, you cannot be long-term missionaries. No, you cannot pursue every exciting thought that goes through your head. No, you cannot quit everything and travel the world.

Men tend to run off excitement while women with children dial in the needs of the marriage and kids into their decisions. That is a good and godly boundary.

Look, I am not advocating neutering you as a dad. God's boundary lines are not the same as a culture that seeks to domesticate us into spermless males. He is up to good for your entire family, including you. God's guidance has to do with timing, not killing the thrill of living.

God is the Father of adventure and will lead us into an adrenaline-filled abundant life. But not every day is a day to jump off the cliff. Some seasons we are called to stay the course, because He is providing something for us later down the road in His perfect time.

A KITE WITHOUT A STRING

Boundaries are like kites with strings.

A kite without a string is just a piece of paper thrown around by the wind. They soar for a moment, then crash down hard, torn to pieces to never fly again. Strings allow kites to fly high, harnessing the power of the wind.

A life without boundaries is a kite without a string—great potential but destined for a painful, sporadic, up and down life. God's plan for you is steady expansive growth within parameters.

You don't blow up God's boundary lines to get what you think you want faster. You don't pull the pin on the grenade. You don't cut your kite string thinking now you are really free as you fly untethered into the unknown. You may soar high and out of sight for a season, but we will find you down the road somewhere stuck in a tree torn to pieces.

God is not withholding, restricting, or limiting your life to teach you a lesson. His intention is not to make you the poster boy for #martyrlife magazine. God desires to give you a gift. He says yes to the deepest desires of your heart. Irrespective if you know them or not at the time, He does.

"For no matter how many promises God has made, they are 'Yes' in Christ" (2 Cor 1:20a, NIV).

STAY ON THE TRAIL

One of the simple pleasures in my life these days is trail running. My Siberian Husky Scout is my running buddy. He warns me if there are snakes on the trail, which there are many in the summertime.

Huskies are notorious for running away. So I keep him on leash when I run.

One morning he gave me grief as we started our run. I thought his harness pinched him. I took the harness off for a moment to adjust it, and he got away.

The look in his eyes was like a crazy kid in front of a jar full of candy. He tore off into the woods like a black and white bolt of lightning. Freaking out, I yelled his name.

My wife and Scout have a tight relationship. Any time he runs off, she fetches him. I tried many times over the years to get him. He does not come to me. Now look at me. Deep in the woods with a wild husky living his best life. He is gone, forever.

Then I heard the still small voice of God. *Get on the trail and he will follow you.* I was torn. I wanted to call him and chase him. To run away from him seemed like a bad idea. I could not shake the impression. So I went with it.

This reminds me of the verse, "Lean not on your own understanding" (Prov 3:5, NIV). God directs us to take actions that are counterintuitive at times.

With reluctance, I started running down the trail in the opposite direction. Sure enough, Scout came in my direction. Darting across the trail, jumping into the lake next to the trail, leaping over fallen trees, and having a blast. I continued to run.

Out of the corner of my eye, I caught a glimpse of him, then he was gone. He never came close enough for me to grab him.

I continued on the trail for a few miles. The whole time I hear God's still small voice, *Stay on the trail and he will come back to you.*

Then a miracle happened. My wild husky fell in line right behind me on the trail as I continued to run. I did not stop and try to grab him.

I kept running, in shock.

God began to speak to me. *Your children are like Scout. They are faster than you. They pivot and change directions on a dime. They explore and venture out beyond the trail. They are having the time of their lives.*

You know the feeling of complete freedom as a kid. The only agenda for the day is fun. You don't have a care in the world.

Then God brought up a conversation I had with Him years ago.

As a younger dad, I complained to God about my life. I asked God to let me go, let me loose. I had energy, passion, creative ideas, and desires to do way more than be a tech monkey.

My kids were young, and we were in full family mode. Except for me. *My job doesn't appreciate me. I'm not living up to my maximum potential of what I could do and be in life.* Super frustrated and restless, I complained to God.

At the time, God told me, *Stay the course.* Stay in your current job, at your current house, in your current city, with your current church. Stay on the trail.

Pour into your kids. Put time and energy into them versus your own grand plans. I did not want to hear it. For years, I approached God about making a change in my life, His response was always the same, *Stay the course.*

On the trail with Scout, God asked me a question. *Do you see why I told you no for years?*

Sweat poured down my face as I slowed down.

He continued, *Staying the course provided a home for your children to come back to.*

I pondered His words as I ran, dodging snakes.

I thought about all the ideas I had as a young dad. All I wanted was adventure and risk. I was not interested in lawn maintenance, PTAs, and HOAs. To live life on the edge in adventurous places, like the jungles of Africa, feet over the deck of a sailboat in the Indian ocean. Move to LA to pursue acting for film and television. Start a worldwide missions organization. Be a pastor. Pioneer missions teams to unreached tribes. Pursue a music career as I had been a singer/songwriter. Move our family to Ethiopia and extend the gospel to the oppressed country of Eritrea. Be an artist, writer, speaker. Produce a kids' TV show based on characters my wife and I created called Dirty Sock and Sally. Kathy played a kindergartener who forgot to take her ADD meds, and I played a sock puppet with a bad attitude. We mixed in Bible lessons and Saturday Night Live humor.

None of those dreams ever came true.

Thank God.

The instability and anxiety in me as a result of pursuing all these ideas would have been through the roof. I was not strong enough as a dad to handle financial and emotional uncertainty. My stress levels would have led to angry outbursts, I guarantee it. Looking back, my faith was too weak and underdeveloped to trust God that much. Yet I was too prideful to admit it at the time.

There is nothing wrong with desiring an epic life of thrills and adventure. Following God is all of this, but it may come in a way you don't recognize. God's will for me was to learn to become a father and a husband. To build a legacy. To change generations to come in my own household. I sought to become like my pioneer missionary and ministry heroes, Loren Cunningham, Brother Andrew, Jim Elliot, Franklin Graham, Bob Pierce, Don Richardson, Ress Howell, Hudson Taylor, and David Livingstone. Those pursuits only lead to personal frustration.

Looking back, thank God, He told me no. I was a spiritually charged unstable mess. My undiscovered diagnosis only made matters worse. My family needed stability. I needed stability.

Spending years in counseling seeking wholeness and mental and emotional health taught me to value small improvement over time. I sought to be a great man overnight, in a spiritual meeting or a single encounter with God. Yet my inner world continued in turmoil after the high wore off. Greatness starts within, then is revealed. It takes time depending on where you start in life. Be patient with yourself. I thought changing circumstances on the outside would change my inner world. It did not. God does not work from the outside in but from the inside out.

Had I pursued my lofty goals as I younger dad, I would have blown up my family, my marriage, and my life.

Now here I am many years later. Slower, less intense, less energetic, fewer creative ideas, less stamina, yet my heart is full. Overflowing with gratitude, not regret, for the decision I made. God made me into a strong and stable man. Someone my loved ones can depend on and a pillar in our home. Me a pillar? God indeed works miracles.

Years of God telling me no. Years of God telling me to stay the course has led me to this place. My wild children can venture out. Run amuck if you will. They always have a place to come home to. In their crazy world, there will always be the slow and steady of mom, dad, and home.

BUILD HOME

God gave me a gift more profound than granting my every desire for an adventurous life.

What I asked God for was an epic life for me, personally. What God did was build an amazing home, an epic family. A home that endures through generations. A tribe of mothers, fathers, sons, and daughters who love God. A family who loves each other and thrives in life.

All the while I'm moaning to God about my unfulfilling tech career. How I could be more and do more. Unaware of the gift. God gave me my deepest heart's desire. A godly and loving family. Not just for today but for future generations. He set the foundations. He established the pillars. He built me into the man I am today over years of training. He desires to do the same with you.

Isn't that what you want? To live a life that really matters to those closest to you for years into the future. God is telling you no today. So He can tell you yes to the deeper more meaningful things you long for in life. Things more valuable than money, accolades, or adventure. He wants to give you your heart's desire to love and be loved for years to come.

God is looking for men to start a legacy with. A watershed man who will do the hard work to stop the generational sins from being passed down any more. A man who will follow God radically even if it means living an obscure life. With God there is always more than meets the eye. We are raising kings and queens in unassuming households.

CHAPTER 17
BE AWESOME
WITH GOD, NOTHING IS IMPOSSIBLE

IT IS A HIGH AND HOLY CALLING TO BE A DAD. A MINISTRY, IF YOU want to use those terms. For years, I missed the good God was up to in my life because I looked for it in the wrong direction. Throughout my life, He pointed me home. My mission was not out there but right here where my family and I lived.

Twenty years ago, a prophet spoke to me in front of the church when Kathy and I first arrived in Raleigh.

"I want you to know, my son, I have brought you here to establish in you the Fatherhood of God and my love for you.

I have brought you here not only to establish you in My Father-hood, but to make you a father.

I am not only bringing you here for a season, says the Lord. This is home to you and I am going to establish you in My Father-hood. I am going to Father you here. I am going to make up what was lacking in your fathering, says the Lord.

I am going to speak into the most sensitive issues of your life. You have been scared to death you wouldn't be a good father and a good husband. You feel something is going to hound you and pound

*the two of you. That somehow you wouldn't make it and somehow
you would be a betrayer. I want to know I am breaking that off
of you.*

I am proud to call you My son."

God did and continues to do what He promised. He made up for
what was lacking in my parenting. He took me by the hand and guided
me every step. I am the dad I am today because I had the best Father a
man could ever have, God.

TURNING 50

I've been on some type of medication for bipolar II for the last nine
years. It took me years to accept that I take medication. I am at peace
about it today.

I have gone low. I reaped the rewards of staying there. I endured and
won the race many lose because it requires too much of them. My testimony of a story of humility over time reaps great benefits for all involved.

The great irony of all this is I've grown weaker, not stronger.

I started our marriage strong in my own eyes. Strong in vision.
Strong in personality. Strong in opinion. Strong in faith. Strong in leadership. Now all these years later, I am weak.

I take medication. I am unsure of myself. I am meek in personality
by comparison. I am less confident. I question if I hear God correctly. I
need my wife's help in many areas of my life. I am below the radar. I am
anonymous, unknown, and obscure.

Yet, I've never been higher. From this place of weakness, I receive
supernatural strength. There is no other way to obtain it.

I was so afraid of being weak for years, thinking life was all up to
me. But I know I need God. I need His loving intervention. I am not
to go it alone.

Today, I can say I jumped off the cliff with God and lived to tell
about it. I went down roads I never wanted to go down. Paths of humiliation, medication, gut-wrenching honesty, true confessions before my

wife and children, requests for help from others, and living in God's light exposed me for who I really was.

I am better and my family is better for all of it. I would not change my story if God handed me the pen.

This last year, I celebrated my fiftieth birthday. It was a day of honor when it could have easily been a day of disgrace, a milestone of regret. My wife and children created a piece of artwork to hang on the wall. Across the top it reads the fifty reasons why we love you. It is one of my most prized possessions.

I will share what my kids and wife wrote about me not to indulge a *me* fest but to encourage you. No matter how far you've fallen, through humility and endurance, you can win the race God set before you.

You can win it because you were made to cross finish lines that you cannot even see right now. With hands raised, you will emerge the victor and the champion. You will become the dad God created you to be.

50 reasons why we love you . . .
you lead by example
you love us unconditionally
you take care of us
you are always there to help
loving father
loving husband
you are strong
you are kind
you are generous
you are a great mentor
you make me coffee every morning
you fight for what you believe in
you are full of integrity
you are courageous
you put Jesus first
you are not a quitter

you are wise
you are the coolest dude I ever meet
you are faithful
you have a heart to inspire us to be who God made us to be

I will end with portions of a letter from Avi, my oldest son. I tear up every time I read it.

"I am so honored and blessed to call you 'Dad.' In today's world, it feels like the role of a father has been diminished, but I'm proud to say I have a father who has embodied what it means to be a dad by never giving up on life, continually living with passion, leading by example, and raising some awesome kids. You inspire me to take risks, be myself, go after my dreams, and grow with the Lord. I always know I have you when I need advice or guidance. You are never too busy to spend time with me. I hope I can even be half as awesome as you when I have my own youngins'. Even when I have messed up bad, you have always been there to remind me of who I am and what God says I am. Love you, Pops."

I pray you can walk your own path of endurance and humility with God at your side, so one day you can receive such a reward from those who know you the best. All the years I thought God was trying to destroy me. I thought He was stripping every part of who I was until there was nothing but a heap of ashes left.

My heavenly Father was giving me the greatest gifts a man could ever ask for: honor, respect, and love from those who know me best.

I was once a mentally unstable man. A physically abusive father. An emotionally abusive husband. A rageaholic.

I listened to Seth's advice to go low. I trusted my wife when she said I needed help. I did not accomplish any of this as an isolated, arrogant, "I've got this, and I don't need you" kind of man. I walked openly with close spiritual brothers for years as I worked it out.

I obtained honor through going low and staying there. In due season, God lifted me up. God restored my marriage. God recovered my relationships with my kids.

God trained me as a dad to go low, to endure, and to win in what matters the most in life.

I am living proof of the Scripture, "Humble yourselves before the Lord, and he will lift you up in honor" (James 4:10, NLT).

AN ARMY OF FATHERS

Let me wrap up our little expedition into dadhood with some sage advice from the American sitcom, *How I Met Your Mother*.

> *"When I am sad, I stop being sad and be awesome instead! True story."*
> —*Barney Stinson*

Like me, you may have every reason in the world to back away for active fatherhood. Faceplants weigh you down. Don't be disheartened.

It can be hard, but it is not impossible. My life is a testimony.

"Jesus said to them, 'With people this is impossible, but with God all things are possible'" (Matt 19:26, NASB).

Wrap your brain and belief around that. All things are possible. In the original Greek it means *all*. I dropped out of seminary but I picked that one up on the way out. A couple of caveats. Not all things today. Not all things you immediately want.

But don't be sad about it, be awesome instead.

With God, timing is everything. Wise warriors are patient and look for the right opportunity. He will direct you when to engage and when to wait.

When God opens a window of opportunity in your marriage, with your children, seize the moment.

Don't force change with family meetings and other formal approaches to try to speed up the improvement process. Trust me, it will backfire. Your family is not a problem to solve but a mystery to enter into. God has plans for each member including you. Look for His guidance on how to move the ball forward one day at a time.

Some days you will faceplant but rest assured, "No weapon formed against you will prosper" (Isa 54:17, NIV).

The Bible says, the demonic offensive plays against you will decline, wither, fall, stagnate, and die.

- "The LORD will grant that the enemies who rise up against you will be defeated before you. They will come at you from one direction but flee from you in seven" (Deut 28:7, NIV).

- "The LORD's enemies . . . will go up in smoke" (Ps 37:20, NIV).

- "I pursued my enemies and overtook them; I crushed them so that they could not rise; You made my adversaries turn their backs in flight, and I destroyed my foes. I beat them as fine as dust" (Ps 18:37–38, 40, 42a, NIV).

- "We are more than conquerors through him who loved us" (Rom 8:37, NIV).

You are a warrior and a king in the making. You are raising kings and queens.

God is looking for a dad to start a legacy with. You are the man he is looking for. He is the Dad you need for the journey into fatherhood.

I will end with the rest of what God shared with me when He told me to hold the heart of my children tenderly many years ago. He gave me a glimpse into today.

"Through you, Troy, the breaches in the wall will be closed. Fatherless sons will become my fathers for generations to follow."

In response, I prayed, "God, use the very baseball bat Satan tried to use against me, on him. Use me to raise up a generation of fathers who will overcome the evil one all around the world."

In your hands, you hold the fulfillment of God's word to me and my prayer. You are a part of the army of fathers that He will raise up to overcome. No more breaches. Trained by God. A father to future generations.

A man who will be awesome, instead. True story.

ACKNOWLEDGMENTS

Allen Arnold, Writing Coach
This book would not exist without Allen Arnold's tough love as my writing coach. I wanted to keep my story in the shadows and just focus on the lessons learned in the back half of the book. Being an intuitive, experienced, and wise writing coach, he challenged me to be vulnerable and "go there." As a result, every reader has an honest account of the journey God took me on and will take them on to become the fathers they are called to be. Thank you, Allen. I owe you my deepest gratitude.

Natalie Hanemann, Editor
Natalie was the first outsider to see the "janky" manuscript that was my first draft. There was work on every page. The quality of book it is now is the direct work of her expertise. I want to thank Natalie for believing in the project and seeing the value for other dads in the early stages. Thank you for making this book readable and enjoyable.

Igor Milhomens, Graphic Designer
Igor has an excellent eye for cutting-edge lifestyle designs. He is great to work with and always produces innovative ideas with very little direction. I am so thrilled his design captured the spirit of adventure and risk-taking this book represents.

Lorie DeWorken, Book Designer
Lorie brought the internal portion of the book to life. She brought key design elements and page layout that moved the book from words on a page to words that came alive. As a self-published author, I deeply appreciated her attention to detail and for bringing a wow factor to the manuscript.

ABOUT THE AUTHOR

Troy Mangum is an author, speaker, podcaster and men's advocate. He is also a Lumbee Indian tribal member. Troy lives in Raleigh, North Carolina with his wife Kathy. He has two sons, two daughters, and one son-in-law.

A former YWAM missionary, hardcore punk singer, substance abuse counselor, busker, long boarder, exotic fruit farmer, vert skater, singer-songwriter, software engineering manager, traveling hitchhiker, and seminary dropout.

CONNECT WITH
TROY

TROYMANGUM.COM

@TROY__MANGUM

LISTEN TO
PODCAST

THE
KINDLING
FIRE

THEKINDLINGFIRE.COM

A CAUSE **CLOTHING BRAND**

friend

BETRUETHREADS.COM

BUY 1 GIVE 1 TO A LOCAL DOMESTIC VIOLENCE SHELTER

TRAINING YOUNG MEN

IN THE ANCIENT PATHS OF MASCULINITY

JER. 6:16-17

HOCOKA

HOCOKAMEN.COM

@HOCOKAMEN

BE A PART OF SENDING
FAMILIES TO THE NATIONS

CALEBWOULDGO.COM